DISCARD

WRITING JUVENILE STORIES
AND NOVELS

WRITING JUVENILE / STORIES AND NOVELS

How to write and sell fiction for young people

By Phyllis A. Whitney

Publishers   THE WRITER, INC.   Boston

Library of Congress Cataloging in Publication Data

Whitney, Phyllis A.   1903-
    Writing juvenile stories and novels.
    1. Children's stories—Authorship.   I. Title.
PN3377.W53   1976   808.3   76-3581
ISBN 0-87116-098-6

Printed in the United States of America

CONTENTS

ACKNOWLEDGMENTS

I wish to thank my good friend Roland West for drawing upon his long experience as a children's librarian to enrich my chapter on "Specialization" with titles and comments that will be valuable to the reader.

My thanks also to the many students in my classes over the years for all *they* have taught me.

INTRODUCTION

This book has been written by two rather different people. One was a young woman writing in the forties (who did not regard herself as young). Some portions of the book belong to that Phyllis Whitney, and I am amazed in reading them now to discover how smart she was and how much she knew about writing, even though she had written only five books. She was also close in time and experience to other beginning writers, and that was an advantage that has been preserved in this new volume.

The second collaborator is a woman writing thirty years years later (who does not regard herself as old), and who has some fifty-five published books to her credit. She bears the same name, of course, but is not really the same person. Life and experience have matured her, though they have not taught her to love living any the less. Perhaps she knows a little more now and has further developed her writing talents, so there are many things she wants to say from her present vantage point.

In reading the book, you won't always know which one of us is speaking, since there is an interweaving of experience, all the way through. But sometimes you will find the present Phyllis Whitney stepping openly onstage to disagree with, or support, the younger one. I hope this won't be too disconcerting, as I don't believe the book could be honestly written in any other way than to give both of us a voice.

The technical side of writing and the matter of being a

writer have changed hardly at all over the years, and I am pleased to discover that I have followed most of my own advice in my growth as a writer. Possibly, this could be why my books are popular today and my name is well known in the field I have chosen. These techniques and devices *work*. All but four of my books are still in print, so it's likely that I've been doing something right.

In this new volume, there had to be much updating because of changes in our world and in our young people during the last thirty years. This is no longer a time of innocence—though we didn't think we were all that innocent *then!* I can remember when a character in a novel by John Tunis said "damn" right out loud, and there was a furor when the book appeared.

Today, there is no longer the censorship which existed in the children's field at mid-century and before. Or perhaps we now have a different sort of censorship. I regret to say that almost anything goes today. It may be that we are more honest or at least that is what we claim—or possibly we have lost something in giving up childhood so much earlier. I don't really know, and in any case, it can't be helped.

I do know that storytelling has been my job and that I still get letters from young readers telling me I am their "favorite" author. These letters refer as often to a book written twenty-five years ago as to one published last year. So that is what this book is all about—the sort of storytelling that enables the reader to experience and feel—and perhaps to learn. Always to enjoy.

I hope this collaboration between two of the women I've been in my lifetime will continue to inform and encourage new writers. I hope they will go on sending letters to tell me when I've helped them, as readers of the earlier book on writing juvenile fiction have been doing for so many years. This is my chance to say "thank you." Both collaborators are grateful.

—PHYLLIS A. WHITNEY

WRITING JUVENILE STORIES AND NOVELS

1 | WHY WRITE FOR CHILDREN?

One of the first lessons the writer of young people's stories and novels must learn is a hard one. However bravely and hopefully he sets out, however much he may respect his audience and believe in the worth and importance of what he is doing, he will find almost at once that his efforts, whether published or not, will be looked upon with condescension by friends, by other writers, and in fact by anyone who is not actively concerned with children.

Make no mistake about it, this attitude, until you become immune to it, can sting. It is one of the penalties you will have to pay in return for the many rewards which come to those who write for children. Apparently the general idea seems to be that after a while you will "grow up" and turn out something respectable and dignified and important like an adult novel.

Finally, to prove I could do it, I wrote a "grownup" book. It was a murder mystery, and, if the reviewers were right, not too bad a job. After it was published a well-meaning lady came up to me one day.

"I understand you've written a mystery novel," she said. I admitted that I had.

"It's a grownup book, isn't it?" she persisted.

Again I admitted the unhappy truth.

She nodded approvingly. "Isn't that fine! You're going

ahead now. One of these days you'll be writing something *significant.*"

I decided that the next time I looked about for a victim for a murder mystery, I would make this woman my first choice. Since that time, I have written many adult novels, but I know I will never want to leave the juvenile field. Whatever novels of "significance" I may still write will be for young people.

My romantic suspense novels for the adult market are fun in a different way, but they are also very hard work. I find, however, that it rests me to turn from one field to another and that I have less inclination to go stale if I can find variety in my writing. Of course, in the adult book market there is always the possibility that one may reach the best-seller list, achieve serialization here or abroad, or be selected by one of the book clubs. There are greater limitations on earnings in the juvenile field, but there are also special rewards, and the possibility of increasingly steady earnings.

Since you who are reading this book are contemplating a career in writing for children, let's have a look at some of these rewards and find out how worthwhile they are.

Perhaps the greatest of all is the satisfaction of writing for an audience still plastic in character. Too often with adults the pattern is so firmly set after twenty that you can do very little about it. Give a grownup a book concerning some controversial subject and what reaction are you likely to get? If the book agrees with what he believes, he will tell you it is a good book. If it disagrees, he'll tell you how bad it is. But chances are that his opinions are so jelled that he will resist any effort to change them. It isn't that his plight is hopeless or that he can't change, but rather that as people grow older they are inclined to cling more and more to accustomed ruts of thinking, so that nothing short of a devastating upheaval will pry them loose from an opinion, however antiquated. This may not be true of all adults, but it is certainly true of many. With young people, the flexibility has not yet been lost.

One of the most touching things about youth is its eagerness to learn, to grow, to find a better way. Today there is much greater concern for the world and its troubles than existed in the past, and this concern begins at a younger age. Today's writers for young people try to meet this concern with honesty and directness.

Such writers have an almost frightening responsibility. Writing for children is not something to be approached lightly or blithely, with no regard for the effect of the words upon your readers. Good fiction can carry an emotional impact that may be very strong. For the writer there can be great satisfaction in creating stories for this eager audience and in reaching them with whatever truths you wish to convey.

Bear in mind, however, that while these readers are eager to learn and grow, many of them today are less than eager to *read*. Too many young people grow up passively watching television, where effort and skill are not required. So, if you are to reach young people at all and persuade them of the joy and satisfaction of meeting characters on a printed page, *your* skill must be greater than ever.

I am afraid I have little patience with writers who write to please only themselves. If you have nothing to give or to say that the world wants, what good are you as a writer? A writer must be worth reading, and it is quite likely that if no one wants to read what you write, you, and not the world, may be wrong.

It is also necessary in our kind of world to earn a living, and it is admirable enough to want that living to be the best we can possibly make it and still retain our integrity.

In no field of writing are the monetary rewards likely to be immediately abundant. Don't, whatever you do, give up all else upon receiving your first check and set out to earn your way by writing. A great many people earn a very good living by writing alone, but earning ability comes slowly, as it does in any other vocation. You must establish yourself, become known in your field, find regular markets where you can repeat with more sales, and perhaps find ways of supplementing the income you earn from your fiction.

While competition in the juvenile field is keen, the chances for the beginner to break in are reasonably good; editors are ready to help, and there are several short story markets which may accept and publish your fiction, though payment is low.

In the book field, the picture is more encouraging. Book markets are numerous, and editors are eager to discover the new writer who shows real promise. Your earnings in the book field may not rank with the nearest best seller, but few books become best sellers anyway, compared to the number published in a year. The average juvenile is almost sure to pile up more impressive sales than the average, non-best-selling novel. Adult novels are, sadly, short-lived. Three months, four months, rarely more than six, and the sales drop to nothing, the book goes out of print. But the juvenile book, while it may not pile up sales spectacularly in the first months of publication, goes quietly on selling year after year, earning the author a steady income. Put a few books behind you and the earnings increase from year to year, even during droughts when no new book is published. Juvenile books are kept in print far longer than adult novels and are apt to go into edition after edition as the years run on. It is not at all uncommon to hear from some writer of juveniles that a book published eighteen or twenty years earlier is still earning royalties.

The adult novel by an unknown writer rarely reaches the 10,000 mark in copies sold, and the ten percent royalties don't add up to a great deal of money. In the children's field, sales run higher over the years, and if a book is well received, libraries keep wearing out copies and buying more.

Taking a look at the overall picture, one must recognize that earnings in the juvenile writing field are not likely to purchase yachts and Hollywood swimming pools in any great hurry. If you train yourself to be a steady producer, if you so organize your working time that you make the best of whatever hours you can arrange for writing, you can earn a modest income. As you become established, you can run that income up to a respectable figure, depending on your own ability, and ingenuity, and industry.

Probably, however, if you have a real bent for writing for children, you will not consider these things first. You will be likely to react as do the artists who produce the beautiful illustrations often found in children's books. Any artist will tell you that illustrating children's books is not particularly lucrative when you compare the amounts received from publishers with the fees paid for artwork in commercial advertising. Yet, children's books never want for the best in artwork.

So you, too, will write for children because that is what you want to do, because that is what you most enjoy doing. You will turn a deaf ear to the people who ask when you are going to write that "grownup book." You will suffer the usual rejection-slip fever, the discouragement and disappointment that are part of the beginner's lot. You will stay with your appointed task grimly and doggedly, until the awkwardness of using new tools wears off, and one exciting day you take into your hands a magazine carrying your first printed story, or you unwrap a copy of your first book. And when, some weeks or months later, a child writes you a letter or tells you enthusiastically in person that your book is wonderful, you wouldn't change places for anything in the world with the author of this year's adult best seller.

2 | LET'S TALK ABOUT YOU

We have been talking about the pros and cons of writing for children. Now let's talk about you, the writer. What are your qualifications? What are your assets and handicaps? What have you to bring to this particular field of writing? Or to any field of writing?

Perhaps you are not yet sure whether you want to specialize in writing for children. That's all right, too. It is just as well in the beginning to try your hand at various types of writing until you find the right and most comfortable niche for you. One word of warning—don't take up writing for young people because it seems easy and you mean to use it as a training ground or stepping-stone to some other field.

Writing for young people is a job for specialists. It is not simple but requires the best you can give it. When you have served your apprenticeship in the juvenile field you will have learned *how to write for children.* Although a great many rules and basic writing techniques apply to all kinds of writing, if you intend to use writing for children only as a stepping-stone, you would be better off serving your apprenticeship in the field for which you really want to write.

Writing for children will not spoil you for other kinds of writing, but it is *different.* Experiment and find out where you belong. It isn't necessary to write only for children, though you may find yourself happy doing that. After some years of writing juveniles, I discovered that I didn't want all my eggs in one basket, and I began to alternate between young people's and adult books—just as I had done from the beginning in writing short stories. However, after you have passed the experimental stage and have tried everything, it is a good idea to keep writing a special type of book long enough to build a following or readership. If you write all kinds of books, you will not find readers who wait for each of your books to come off the press. In the case of almost any well-known writer, you will find readers who count on a certain type of story from his typewriter, and he continues to give it to them. This is the way to gain readers and build sales over the years.

Let's look now at some of the qualities you will need to have (or to develop) if you are going to succeed in any field of writing.

How is your vitamin content? Because you're going to need energy, energy, energy. Not perhaps the kind of energy it takes to dig a ditch or win a game of ping-pong, but energy all the same. There are times when a hard stint of sitting at a typewriter will leave you as worn out, mentally and physically, as if you had put in a day at hard labor. I remember writing a twelve-page chapter about an exciting basketball game and doing it all at one sitting. When I got up from my desk, I was as limp with weariness as if I had actually made every play in that game personally.

Nevertheless, this is the type of energy that even invalids can sometimes manage. Robert Louis Stevenson is only one of the many writers who achieved a prodigious output in spite of ill health. And I have known individuals who bounced with good health and still could not take the grind of sitting at a typewriter because it so tired them.

Next, how is your courage? Perhaps the major requirement of a writer is a strong backbone and the kind of chin that can take it—not once, but again and again. If you pride yourself on your "sensitivity," if you curl up and die when some brute expresses a low opinion of your brainchild, if you get your feelings hurt easily—well, I won't say you can't be a writer. But I certainly will say that you won't be a very good one until you take yourself in hand and toughen up. You can, you know.

What are these things you'll have to learn to take? Rejection slips, of course. So what if your first three masterpieces don't sell? What if your first thirty don't? Or what if you sell one story with ease and after that you write nothing but failures for months? Can you keep going back to your typewriter? Can you hang on with the kind of grim determination that will not be beaten down?

I am sure I can point to a great many writers (myself among them) who started out with more determination than talent. And I can point to brilliant flash-in-the-pan writers who haven't the ability to plod and stick with it through inevitable discouragement. They fall by the way-side, while the rest of us, who may not really write as well, keep ourselves a steady course until we eventually succeed.

In my own case, it took me four years from the time I first mailed out a story to an editor to make my first sale. In three more years, I sold three more stories. That adds up to seven years and four stories sold. Can you take it to that extent? Let me add, by way of comfort, that you probably won't have to. I am an unusually horrible example, and if I were a centipede I couldn't have gotten off on more wrong feet. Records I have kept from the beginning show that I wrote more than three hundred short stories and sold fewer than one hundred. Then I discovered that I was really a book writer, and after one failure in the children's book field, I wrote a juvenile book that sold—and I have been selling ever since. It is all very well to have your eyes on the stars, but much wiser to keep your feet moving step by step along the path that leads to the stars instead of trying to cover the distance all in one jump. When you find the type of writing you most want to do, don't start out by taking aim at the top market in that field. That is a waste of time, unless you're a genius. If you are, you won't be reading this book, because you will know all about the subject without my help. But if you're just an ordinary guy or gal who wants to write salable fiction, have a try at the less glittering markets which may possibly be interested in your writing while you are in the process of learning your craft. You're not ready for that spotlight act and probably won't be for a while.

Let's say you have energy, courage, determination. Patience is another quality you'll need. Patience to take endless pains over small details. Patience to rewrite. Patience to wait. Just plain patience.

Next, how are you when it comes to budgeting your time? Oh, so *that's* your trouble! You are full of energy, courage, determination and patience, but you simply do not have any time. Your head is filled with story ideas, and some day you are going to get them down on paper. Some day when you have time.

You are just the person I want to talk to. It may surprise you to know that nobody else has any time either. Look at successful people in any line of work, and you'll find that the thing they have less and less of with every passing year is time.

Time is not something you "have." It is not even something you "find." It is something you *make*. You make it forcibly by pushing other things out of the way. Other things you want to do; even other things you ought to do.

Yes, I know. You work all day in an office. You're all worn out when you come home at night. By the time dinner's over, there really isn't any time. And on Saturday you have to wash clothes, or wash the car, or do the marketing. And on Sunday—well, you have to have some fun, don't you?

Or you don't work in an office. You are a housewife. Anybody knows that keeping house is a full-time job. And besides, there are the children. How can anybody write with kids running around, getting into trouble, getting hurt, getting sick, asking questions? After all, your job as mother comes first. When the baby is a little older, perhaps; or when Johnny gets started at school. . . .

Don't fool yourself. If you belong to the I-haven't-the-time category, you'll never have time. The office job will keep taking more and more out of you; the children will prove more difficult as they grow older; and when the current reasons for not having time run out, you'll be able to find plenty of new ones, all equally logical and impressive. There's your emotional state, for instance. Have you tried that? With all these dreadful things going on you are simply too upset to write. This works in connection with anything, from the news in today's paper, to the fact that your husband didn't kiss you goodbye when he went to work this morning.

Nonsense! If you want to write, you'll make time. If you don't want to, you'll manage to rationalize yourself out of really getting to it.

I know plenty of writers, both men and women, who work all day and still manage to make time to write. And sell what they write. Every one of them hopes to reach that happy state where writing will earn more than the job, so that they can give up the job and "have time to write." Meanwhile, they are doing a wonderful job of budgeting whatever time they can make—whether it means getting up an hour earlier in the morning, or sitting inside all day on

Sunday, or fitting in an hour at the typewriter every night.

I know women who write straight through having babies, and afterwards, while the children are growing up. Instead of doing their household chores first thing in the morning as many women do, perhaps they put it off until late in the afternoon. They, too, dream of the day when they'll "have time." In the meantime, they are busy making it, and those checks that come in take care of Johnny's tonsils, or buy Susy's new shoes, and sometimes they even buy the writer a new coat.

Then, at what the story writers used to call "long last," the time comes when these industrious little workers begin to make their writing pay. Oh, happy day! The news that he is losing a valued employee is broken to the boss. And somebody is hired to scrub the floors at home. Isn't this jolly? Now we're really going to *have* time to write!

Are we? Don't be funny.

Back to me again. I can live by my writing now; I can give my whole day to it. But I really don't have time to write this book. As a matter of fact, I haven't any business attempting it. I'm doing it only because I remember so well all those years when editors wouldn't pay any attention to me, and now when an editor asks something of me, I'm still so pleased, I can never bring myself to say anything but "yes."

For many years, I worked at outside jobs and wrote when I could snatch the time. Later, I managed to find ways to earn my living at home. I tried everything related to writing in some way. I reviewed children's books, wrote articles, gave lectures, taught writing classes, read manuscripts. But always I kept three hours of writing time in the morning free for my own work. In the yearly records I kept of my total earnings, I used two columns: *Book earnings* was the heading on one; the second column was called *Other*. It was

my long-range hope to have the first column increase sufficiently to let me drop the second. At first the earnings in
the second column were greater, but eventually these
dwindled as my earnings from writing books increased,
until the "Other" column disappeared, except for an occasional entry.

Now that we have discussed a few general qualities you
will need as a writer, suppose we get down to one very special quality you will require if you mean to write for young
people. We could call it the ability to remember.

If you are a woman, what happens when you see two or
three teen-age girls putting their heads together in public?
You watch a while. You see them whisper and giggle and all
talk at the same time. You see them go suddenly off into
peals of laughter, surely out of all proportion to the cause.
How do you react? Do you think, "What idiots!" Or do you
think, "I remember. . . . Once I was like that," and watching
those girls, you can recapture how it feels.

Or if you're a man and you see some boys clowning and
shoving each other around, maybe showing off a little, do
you see them with impatient objectivity, or can you remember what it was like to be that way yourself?

If you're writing for the in-between ages, can you feel the
excitement and interest you want your young readers to
feel? Does that stone Johnny has just turned up look like a
dirty old rock to you, or can you understand how wonderful
it seems to young eyes that have never beheld a stone quite
so remarkable before? Or if you want to write for the very
youngest, can you look at a tree or a toad, a house, a worm,
a city sidewalk, and catch the wonder and excitement that
object gives to the fresh, inexperienced eyes of the littlest
children?

When it comes to emotion, can you understand with your
own feelings what a tragic occurrence the loss of a favorite

marble can be? Can you write about Mary Jane, who hasn't a dress to wear to a dance, and sense the deep hurt this may cause your young heroine?

A great many people really cannot remember how it feels to be young. Those people should certainly never attempt to write for children. If, however, you can regard the tragedies of youth with a sympathy and understanding that do not discount their importance, yet which bring to them the leavening quality of your more mature years and experience, then you have something worthwhile to contribute as a writer. Juvenile fiction is not a field of writing to which you can come carelessly and empty-handed, wondering only what you will get out of it.

There is one more thing.

Once when I had gone into New York to give a talk for the Mystery Writers of America's writing class, I sat in the front row until the first speaker was finished. The woman next to me didn't know who I was, and when the speaker (a well-known professional writer) stepped down, she turned to me and spoke some memorable words: "Did you ever notice something about all these writers who come to talk to us? No matter who they are, not one of them ever tells us the *secret!*"

When I got up to speak, I told her exactly what the secret is—though I doubt if she believed me. And I am going to tell it to you. *You must want to enough.* It's that simple— but think about what those words mean: enough to take the buffeting and the failure while you learn, and sometimes afterwards; enough to pay the price, to say "no" to interruptions, to guard your time, to give up what you might rather do on certain occasions, to work whether you feel like it or not. To stay with it. That's the only secret there is.

3 | WHERE DO YOU BELONG?

Now that we have discussed the whys of writing for children, and the qualities, general and specific, needed by the writer, we are ready to break the field into age groups and find out where you, the individual writer, belong.

Perhaps you already know the age group for which you want to write. In that case, one problem is simplified. Many writers, however, do not in the beginning have any particular bent toward one age group. It may even be that you haven't considered "age groups." "Writing for children" covers the whole subject as far as you are concerned and it may dismay you to find that you must now choose a specific group and keep within the limitations of writing for that group.

If you are undecided, try your hand at writing for different ages, until you find the age with which you are most in sympathy and for which you write best.

In reviewing children's books, I divide them roughly into four age groups: 2 to 6, 6 to 8, 8 to 12, and 12 up. The boundaries for these groups are not by any means fixed and there is a great deal of overlapping. A ten-year-old may sit down most contentedly to read an "easy" book, only to be found the next day with her nose in a book "for 12 up." The six-to-eights often enjoy picture books intended for younger children. It all depends on the reading ability, tastes, and current inclination of the individual child.

In today's market, there is a further shading of boundaries, because children are maturing faster. What I used to write for the 12-up group now brings me mail from the nine- and ten-year-olds. The early teens are reading adult books. The old-fashioned teen-age novels that are still in print are being read by a younger group than was previously the case. There is, however, something now called the Young Adult Novel, and this may deal with young people's problems in today's world and be read by older teens. My own mysteries for the 10–14 group are now appearing in paperback as Young Adult Novels to distinguish them from my adult books, which indicates that age classifications are not rigid.

However, it seems necessary for the sake of bewildered parents and others who cannot always read a book before giving it to a child to suggest some age grouping. These age categories will also be of value to you as a writer, since they will enable you to aim your stories for a specific age level. If older or younger readers also enjoy the novels you have written, that is fine, but they will not be your direct focus while you are writing for your chosen audience.

Writing for each age group has certain advantages and disadvantages which concern the writer. Each has its individual problems; the writer who can comfortably turn out stories for the teens may find himself completely baffled by the picture book technique. Suppose we consider these four groups in order and find out what some of their special problems and requirements are.

PICTURE BOOKS—TWO TO SIX

It is a constant thorn-in-the-side to writers for the older ages that picture books often sell in overwhelmingly greater numbers than books which take much longer to write. In the magazine field, where the writer is often paid by the word, the author of stories for the very young (which may run about 300 words, depending upon the requirements of each magazine) earns considerably less than the one who turns out a 3,500-word story. But in the book field the earnings of the picture-book writer may completely eclipse the earnings of those who write for young people in their pre-teens or teens.

The author of books for teen-agers learns with anguish that some little book of twenty pages and a few dozen words has sold 30,000 copies in a few months, while his own volume of 60,000 words has taken a year to climb to a sale of 5,000. Perhaps he sniffs scornfully and remarks that he ought to give up writing "real" books and get into the picture book "racket."

Fine. Let him try it! As a rule he doesn't, of course, because writing those few dozen words may be completely beyond his power. I am quick to admit that it would be beyond mine. It isn't so easy as it looks. However, *you* may be the one who can do it. If you are, you'll find the field a lucrative one.

The picture book field is one of the most difficult for the new writer to break into because of the increasing costs of production. Such expense can be justified only by what the editors regard as top-quality material. They feel safe with writers and artists who have already succeeded. Nevertheless, new writers must replace the established ones as they get older, and if you have something good to offer, you can still break into print.

We can treat the writing of material for the youngest, whether for the magazine or the book market, as almost the same thing. Sometimes the brief book manuscript gets by on a poorer story, carried to success by the illustrations. For the magazine, the story must be good enough to stand on its own feet.

A story for young people of any age must be written for at least one of several reasons. IT MUST ENTERTAIN. It might be wise for you to print that rule in big letters and tack it up over your desk. Check every story you write against it. If it isn't entertaining, into the wastebasket with it. Other reasons which may motivate your writing of a story are to teach a lesson, or to present information. But never think for one moment that your young readers will want to learn lessons or be informed through reading fiction. If they pick up your story or novel, they do so because they want to be entertained, not preached at. In presenting the manuscript of *Of Human Bondage* to the Library of Congress, Somerset Maugham said, "Fiction is art"; its purpose is "not to instruct, but to please." Well might that be taken for a motto by writers in every field. It is too often forgotten today.

However, you must not write your story only with the interests of your young readers in mind. While you must entertain them, it is adults who buy most books for children. Editors know this and know that certain things have an immediate appeal to those adults. Children may look only for entertainment, but the adult book buyer expects something more. Since it is to the editor (and the adult buyer), then, that you must sell your story, as a writer you will be wise to put into your writing ingredients other than entertainment value.

With the passing years, values and restrictions change. Ours is a freer, more open society. Old barriers are down, old codes laughed at, and there are few taboos. What is known as "frontal nudity" has appeared in picture books, with casual acceptance by the young, who know all about

such things anyway—although it has caused some distur-
bance in older circles.

What taboos are operating are rather different from those
of the past. Words that were unacceptable thirty years ago
are commonplace today, and vice versa. "Negro," for example, is not acceptable now, and "black" must be used
instead. We do not these days tolerate any expression of
prejudice against race, religion or creed in books for children. And we do not indulge in sexism at any age level.
This is a topic I want to discuss later in this book. But in
general avoid in your writing having small girls play only
with dolls, and small boys play only with trucks!

One taboo that still exists at all levels is simply a matter
of common sense. You should not show your young characters doing dangerous things that you don't want your
readers to imitate. Perhaps this is whistling in the dark,
when you consider the examples set on television, but it is
still wise to hold to this standard in writing for children.

The purpose behind a picture book may be to provide
information. A glimpse of another country or a special section of our own country may be shown. Or the picture
book may lead the reader back into history. Sometimes it
merely deals with the familiar—a grocery store, a circus,
a zoo, and so on.

In writing for the very young, the trick of repeating certain words or phrases throughout the story is an effective
one. Marie Hall Ets has used repetition most successfully in
In the Forest. Here the technique is unusual, since the story
of the little boy's walk in the forest is told in the first person. The "I" of the story goes for a walk and meets a great
number of imaginary animals who accompany him until a
grown-up appears on the scene, and they all vanish. The

phrase which becomes a rhythmic refrain is "when I went for a walk in the forest."

While we're on the subject of that walk in the forest, I'd like to insert a warning. Beware of what might be called the "journey story." Marie Ets did it well, but you had better avoid having your young character or animal go out into the world, moving from one plotless incident to another. This type of story has been done to death, and unless it is unusually skillfully handled, the editor won't be interested.

The picture book which tells no story at all but gives factual material in an entertaining manner is enormously popular these days. Nonfiction is somewhat outside the province of this book, but your library will give you examples of hundreds of books about everything from seashells to dinosaurs. Or information may be given in the background of a story and be equally effective. You have the world and all that's in it to draw on for such material.

One of the worries of the beginning writer of picture books is how to get suitable art work for the story. The writer for older children sends in his story manuscript, and the publisher assigns it to an artist if one is required. But what about the writer for the age group where pictures are as important as the story? What does he do about illustration?

The answer is that the picture book story should be good enough to stand on its own, without art work. If it is worth publishing, you can count on the imagination of the juvenile book editor to visualize the possibilities for illustration. Editors have the technical knowledge which most writers lack, including how to handle overall format, page size, length, color printing, and so forth. If you try to have the illustrations done, you may handicap the acceptance of your picture book.

Of course if you know an accomplished artist who wants to try a finished picture and a few roughs to accompany your story, that may be to your advantage. Even then, a completely finished product isn't required, since the editor will prefer a free hand.

As a beginner in this field, you cannot afford to pay the artist ahead of time yourself. You may promise him a share of the royalties if the book sells, but I would not advise going farther than that. He must be willing to take the gamble with you.

Of course if you yourself are an artist and can write your own picture book stories, you can reap a very nice profit in this field, since you will not have to split your royalties with anyone. But first and most important, be sure you learn how to tell a good story, or you will not find a market, no matter how wonderful your drawings.

If your picture book story is accepted and an artist is assigned to it by the editor, you will be expected to share your royalties, as arranged for by contract. If a good deal of art work is needed, 50–50 may be a fair arrangement. A name artist may have the feeling that he has done the lion's share of the work, and the author may have to take a smaller share—40–60 perhaps. But don't forget that if it were not for those few lines of story the book would not exist for him to illustrate. Of course the ideal way is to leave the matter of art work to the editor and accept whatever arrangement can then be worked out. But *first* you have to interest the editor—and I believe that is where we came in.

SIX TO EIGHT

This age group has a less definite pattern than any other. It will contain picture books with longer stories which the beginner may read for himself. Or it may contain "harder" stories which must be read aloud to him.

There has been a good deal of campaigning in recent years for "graded" words. That is, it was felt that in writing for younger children a special vocabulary list was necessary. Obviously, in the picture book group words should be kept fairly simple, but if the *right* word happens to be a big word, I feel that it should be used.

I recommend to anyone who means to write for young people Annis Duff's *Bequest of Wings*. It is a book about one family's adventures in reading and is a real treasure trove for those interested in writing for children. In the chapter called "Fun With Words," the author has this to say:

> I believed then, and I believe even more firmly now, *that all words belong to children*. They choose them for their own use by the simple process of taking possession of the ones they need to express what they want to say. If children do not hear speech that has variety and liveliness, and if their books do not have unfamiliar words tucked in like bright little surprises among the everyday ones, how in the world are they ever to accumulate a store of language to draw on, as new experiences and sensations increase the need and desire to communicate with the people they live with? Children, like the rest of us, need to be articulate, and it seems to me a withholding of what is properly theirs, to limit their choice of words (as in the "vocabulary-tested" book) to the vocabulary already possessed by an "average" child of any given age.

A word of warning might be added here for the writer, however. A great many beginners have a tendency to display their erudition or indulge in what they regard as "fine" writing by using many-syllabled words, where the simple word would be more to the point and more effective. Let's not take the fun of meeting new words out of children's reading, but, on the other hand, let us not write so that an interpreter is needed for every other sentence.

In writing for the six-to-eight reader, the rule of interest first still holds good; any lesson might be less simple and obvious. Information may become more complex and all sorts of interesting matters may be presented in story form. But remember always that you are telling a story and that however fascinating and important you feel the educational side of your work is, it must always be the warp and woof of the story itself, and not superimposed. At the upper range of this age bracket, stories can be longer and the plots fairly complex.

Perhaps the most popular type of story in this age group deals realistically with modern children and their problems. If you have a special feeling for this six-to-eight age group and an interest in its everyday problems, this may be the right place for you. These books also depend heavily on illustrations, but the problem of providing them is the editor's. Here again, you should make your story sufficiently good and worthwhile to interest the publishers, and they will find the right artist to illustrate it.

I am going to say this more than once and I might as well begin now: *Make the problem in your story one that will really interest children.* Keep your own adult interests out of it unless you want to write for adults. I remember a manuscript once submitted to me in a class in which the hero's story problem was to earn enough money to buy books for school. Laudable, indeed, but can you imagine any youngster getting excited about such a project? To buy a bicycle—ah! Or any one of hundreds of other things a boy or girl might like. But out of all the things there are under the sun, this author had to pick school books!

EIGHT TO TWELVE

This age is really fun to write for. There is apparently a greater market for books and stories for eight-to-twelves than for almost any other group. Young people's magazines are interested in publishing stories for this age, and book publishers never seem to get enough. Libraries are always crying for more. As in all these categories, your library will have good current examples.

A point to remember in writing for this group is that children like to read about characters who are older than themselves, or at least as old, so don't make your main character too young.

In the past, a distinction used to be made in this age group between books for boys and books for girls. It was claimed that girls would read "boys' books" but boys would not read books supposedly written for girls; the lines have become fuzzier, and it is probably advisable to mix the two. Though there is no way to avoid having a hero or a heroine, the role each plays is no longer stereotyped.

I do feel, however, that a writer who has a certain story to tell should be allowed to try it his or her way. Restrictions can become crippling. If you feel strongly about a particular story, then go ahead and see what happens. You may succeed, or you may learn a painful lesson.

When I was writing *Willow Hill,* the story of a town in the Midwest that was disturbed by racial conflicts, my regular publisher advised me not to write the book. It was too "dangerous" a subject, it would not sell, etc., etc. I wrote it anyway and entered it in a contest being run by another publisher. *Willow Hill* won first place, but it would never have been written if I had not listened to my own convictions, my own strong urge to say what *I* thought needed to be said. The book has sold very well indeed and is still in print.

Editors do not always know everything.

TWELVE AND UP (OR PERHAPS TEN TO FOURTEEN)

Last of all we have the so-called teen-age group. Many of the books so labeled are read by ten- and eleven-year-olds, but it is simpler to refer to teen-agers. There is also the new category of books and stories for "young adults," which may deal with the problems of youth at a more perceptive, adult level. This does not mean that your main character may not be grown up and out of school. What happens when they finish high school and college interests teen-age readers tremendously. Of course, if your book happens to have the quality of universality, its appeal is unlimited, and older readers will find it for themselves. Books like *Treasure Island* and *Little Women,* for example, are ageless.

This is the most difficult age to write for, which makes these books and short stories every bit as hard to do competently as full-length adult novels or the fiction in major magazines.

Since the time I began to write young people's books, one category that used to exist at this age level has nearly disappeared. Perhaps only in paperbacks are "romances" still thriving and still being read by girl readers and their mothers. You will no longer find books of the sort Janet Lambert and Rosamond du Jardin used to write published in hardcover.

Various types of books come under this age heading. There are still adventure and mystery stories. Science fiction is more popular than ever. Sports stories have fallen off as a special category. Many of these books deal today with racial problems, ghetto problems, unwed mothers, sexual encounters, the homosexual, and all sorts of home problems, including divorce, drinking, parents who have affairs—anything you can name will be found today in books for young adults (who are sometimes only eleven years old!). This is probably a good thing. The wraps are off, and we can speak frankly and honestly to the young about the very troubles some of them must deal with.

It is still not my choice to use four-letter words, though

I have always written about current problems facing young people, and apparently my older books are still not regarded as dated by young readers.

Just remember that first "rule" I gave you. It is every writer's task first of all to interest and entertain. Otherwise, no "lesson" we want to put across will be listened to.

4 | WORKING HABITS

Beginnings are important. Sometimes they are dangerous. If you write your first successful story with your left hand, using an onyx pen and green ink while flying in a plane over South America, you may have a real problem on your hands. Forever after, you may think you can write successful stories only with your left hand, using an onyx pen and green ink, while flying in a plane over South America.

You think that sounds extravagant? It isn't very. I have known writers who have clung persistently to the weirdest, most inconvenient writing habits, simply because a story written under such conditions happened to click. I remember one writer who had to do his early writing while traveling around the country, living in hotels. Hotel desks never suited him, and he contrived some sort of back-breaking arrangement whereby he set his typewriter on a chair and himself on a pile of phone books. Later, when he had his own home and a comfortable desk and chair, he still thought he could not write until he put his typewriter on a chair and sat on a pile of phone books on the floor. It took a lot of reconditioning before he was cured.

I knew another man who had a pair of "writing pants." His despairing wife gave them to the ragman one day, and as a result he could not write for months.

Personally, I have a thing about pencils, and woe betide

anyone who carries off one of my long, pointed pink pencils. What would be regarded by others as "only a pencil" is to me a valued tool, and I want plenty of well-sharpened pink pencils at hand, or I am not comfortable in my writing.

Of course this sort of thing is silly; of course you will do nothing like that! But you'd better watch with a hawk eye in the beginning, until satisfactory writing habits are so ingrained in you that you don't have to worry. You may get the idea that you can write only with a certain pencil, or on a certain kind of paper. Or you may decide that you can't possibly start work each morning until after the mailman comes. Or you have to tidy your entire desk—you could never work looking at a mess like that. Or you have to sharpen pencils, pick lint off the floor, or feed the goldfish and water all the plants.

When these very common symptoms begin to appear, get them in hand at once. If you don't, they'll rule you and waste your time. In this matter you are not dealing simply with your conscious self. You're dealing with a subconscious imp who is a lazy fellow. He knows that once you get to that typewriter he is going to be chained down and forced to work, and he will do everything possible to resist that— until you get him trained. This same imp, once he is harnessed, can be your most helpful assistant, but he has to be shown who is boss.

You must start out by telling him that at nine o'clock in the morning, or at seven at night, or whenever it is that you can write, you are going to sit down and start writing. When that time comes, you do exactly that. You resist all the wonderful distractions with which the imp will supply you at that time, and you start to work. If you give in to him, you'll be sorry, because he can condition you to failure just as easily as you can condition him to working. If, day after day, you fiddle away your working period at odd jobs that ought to be or could be done at some other hour, then you will develop the habit of being a procrastinator instead of a working writer. But if you are persistent, you can train that subconscious imp to such stern, disciplined working habits that when your assigned writing time comes each day, he will give in without a struggle and help rather than hinder you. Once you get him on your side, you can use him in many ways I'll mention from time to time.

Nothing is more important than to set aside a certain period each day for writing. Once you get the habit firmly established, when that time comes you will want to write—just as when mealtime comes you want to eat. How long that writing time will be depends upon you and the circumstances of your life. If you can squeeze in no more than an hour a day, set that hour aside and stick to it.

This will at first entail a certain amount of unpleasantness. Unless you have an unusually understanding and sympathetic family, you are going to find they simply do not consider that writing is "work." It's a nice little hobby for you to have, but how silly to give up everything else in order to do it. Until checks begin to speak impressively, the family is not going to take your desire for solitude at certain hours seriously. But if you don't get them to take it seriously, there aren't going to be any checks.

If you're an old softie who likes to be nice to people— well, go ahead and be an old softie. But don't expect to be a writer. If you want to write, you have to get tough. How you work it out is up to you, depending on your family and your friends. Maybe you'll have to keep a supply of bric-a-brac handy to throw at anybody who opens your door. You will have to snap at the Fuller Brush Man, alienate the affections of your relatives who want to come from California to visit you, make it clear to your friends who call you on the phone that this is your working hour and you will call them back, and otherwise make yourself thoroughly anti-social. Don't worry about losing all your friends. They'll be miffed for a while, but they'll come back. And when you start appearing in print they'll tell *their* friends about how they knew you when.

If you are a man, your problem is simpler because you will be in a better position to retire into solitude and stay there for the required length of time. A woman's lot is harder. If you have a family, you cannot completely bar your door to interruptions; you will not be able to command absolute quiet while you write. But you can learn to write with wild Indians screaming under your window, and you'll find you can distinguish the kind of shriek that means somebody is being killed, from the mere everyday, having-a-good-time kind of shriek. And nothing less than mayhem and murder will take you away from your typewriter. However, you may as well resign yourself to being completely unpopular with your neighbors. If you write in the morning, you will have to make it clear that you cannot permit yourself to stop to listen to a choice bit of gossip whenever someone wants to run in. Rumor will undoubtedly get around that you are a little peculiar. You have to decide if you care more about what people think, or about your writing.

The length of time for which you can comfortably write is something you will have to work out for yourself. It is different for every writer. By experimentation, you will discover what your average wordage output is likely to be and about how much time it will take you to set down that many words. Don't be too easy, push yourself to some extent. But don't expect too much, either, or you may learn to hate the sight of a typewriter.

I work all day long, but not at one writing job. Morning is the best period for me, though for you it may be afternoon, evening, or three A.M. I know writers whose brains don't seem to come alive till after midnight. Since I prefer to write during the morning hours—say from eight to eleven—those are the hours I preserve for the important project in hand. I undertake other writing jobs after lunch. These are not sacred to the laws of non-interruption, as is the writing I do during the morning hours.

During these three hours (sometimes more when I can manage to get to my desk a little earlier) I find that I can comfortably write eight pages—about 2,000 words—as I type. By pushing myself I can write ten pages. When I push and when I take it easy are matters I will talk about in another connection later on. But when I have a project in hand, I try to manage at least eight pages every day. I find it wiser to set myself to a wordage limit rather than a time limit. When you tell yourself you can stop at twelve o'clock, the imp is likely to take over gleefully. "Ah!" he cries. "Nobody says I have to write so many words, or so many pages. All I have to do is sit here till twelve o'clock." And there you are likely to sit, looking out the window, daydreaming, now and then writing a grudging half page. Twelve o'clock comes and you have a page and a half of work to show for the hours you have spent at your machine.

These days I am not quite so grim about it because years of writing have trained and seasoned me. I know I will work and not daydream, so if my eight pages aren't done every day it doesn't matter. Each story scene has its own flow—some faster, some slower.

One of the first things the *writing* writer learns is that inspiration has nothing to do with it. As someone else has pointed out, it is perspiration that counts. You do not wait until you "feel" like writing. Of course there are cycles of productivity. When you are in the enviable state in which words pour out with facility, by all means make the most of it. But don't rely on those periods. They come all too seldom. You write doggedly every day, whether you feel like it or not. And very often, in the final reading, the words you plodded over so reluctantly turn out just as well as those you poured out with ease. But you can push yourself harder during a creative cycle, so take advantage of those periods when they come.

Writers are often asked whether they use pencils or type their manuscripts. When an innocent asks that question in class, some of the others often titter in a slightly superior way. But the question is not so simple-minded as it sounds. This is a matter worth considering. Here again experimentation will reveal the best method for you, though conditioning also plays its part.

Those of us who started writing when we were fairly young probably wrote our first stories in pencil. For a time this may seem the most natural method. When I decided I was going to be a professional, however, I switched to a typewriter. I'd had no business course in school; I used the hunt-and-peck method. For a number of years, I wrote my stories clumsily on my typewriter. Then came a period when I was a semi-invalid for six months and was not allowed to type. I took to propping a bread board against my knees and writing in pencil. I wrote a whole book during that time. (P.S. It didn't sell.) When I was well again, I kept right on using a pencil, having decided that I was more comfortable without the mechanical intricacies of a typewriter taking my attention from the story. And I wrote another book—all in pencil—which *did* sell.

Then something happened to my writing. Production fell off. Sales fell off. Stories came back from my regular markets. I didn't seem to fit in any more. Now I realize that I was going through a transition: I was writing myself out of the short story field into the book field, where I believe

I naturally belong. Until I was willing to accept the change
and acknowledge that I was no longer a short story writer
but a writer of books, I had to go through a grim period
when I seemed to be losing my touch and was getting as
many rejections as I had done in my early years of writing.
The fact that the rejections were now in the form of regret-
ful letters from editors afforded me little comfort. The
word "No" is never accompanied by a check.

Even though I did not fully understand what was happening, I knew I had to take some serious steps. I decided
that for one thing I was making myself too comfortable
while I wrote. I had a big armchair I snuggled into in all
sorts of positions, now holding my friend the bread board
on my lap, now propping it against knees hooked over the
arm of the chair. I found I got sleepy very easily and that I
much preferred to daydream than to write. My subconscious imp took over and encouraged me into lazier and
lazier habits.

But I had not disciplined myself for long years as a writer
for nothing. One day I decided that it was back to the typewriter for me and a complete new conditioning. That is
worth trying if your writing habits have grown sloppy.
Change everything all around. Write in a different room
or at a different hour. Make yourself start over.

This time, however, I did not mean to operate under any
hunt-and-peck handicap. I bought a book of instructions
and exercises on the touch typing method and took two
weeks off from my regular writing to teach myself to type.
I typed exercises for as long as I could bear to sit at the
machine, and in two weeks I had the touch system down. I
could type without watching my fingers, and so could stop
worrying about the mechanics of typing. I certainly was not
very fast at first and probably did things that would make
typing experts shudder—but I learned. And by using a

typewriter, you can certainly write a lot faster without strain. To some pencil-pushers, the threat of writer's cramp is a real one, and though I have never seriously suffered on that score, there were times when I stopped a morning of writing with a hand that ached badly.

For years now I have used a Selectric typewriter with no carriage and a "flying ball" that holds the type. I can type much faster without tiring; it's also true that I can make mistakes a lot faster. For the final copy I now rely on a professional typist, but for a long time editors had to put up with my corrected pages.

It is probably a good idea to be able to write with ease either on the typewriter or with pencil. Occasionally, when some scene sticks and I can't seem to get it right, I will pick up a pencil and scribble it out in longhand. Very often that clears up the difficulty. Also, it is wonderful to be at ease with a pencil when you're away from home. I can write on trains, busses, in automobiles, on restaurant tables. It is a very handy faculty to develop. Most revision I do in pencil.

Before we leave this subject of writing habits, I want to say something about continuous output. I know only too well the system the beginner is likely to follow, because it used to be mine. I would spend weeks getting around to writing a story. Then, with all the appropriate birth pangs, I would produce my masterpiece. Every word was precious to me. I was confident that it was going to lead me to publication—and, of course, fame and fortune. I sent it off with high hopes and then sat down to wait, surely for a check this time.

Of course I couldn't possibly get my mind on another piece of work until I knew my story's fate. The magazine to which I had mailed the story had a couple of others to read besides mine, and it took anywhere from two weeks to two months to get an answer. During this time, I twiddled my thumbs and waited. (The imp was on vacation, having a wonderful time and encouraging me to follow *his* inclination and do nothing.) Then, sooner or later, back came the manuscript, accompanied by a printed slip which explained that no reflection was being cast upon the worth of my story, *but*. . . . In other words, *"No."* This shock devastated me so completely that I couldn't write at all for at least another six weeks, during which time I licked my wounds, suffered, and knew I would never in this world have another idea for a story.

I didn't know any writers; I had no one to take me by the scruff of the neck and give me a good shaking. There was no one to say, "Look here, my friend, the first thing you need to learn is the professional attitude."

What is the "professional attitude"? It's just this. The minute you have a story off your hands, abandon it. It is no longer the apple of your eye, for you have given your fickle affections to a brand-new apple that you had your eye on perhaps even before you finished the last story. Off with the old and on with the new. And no vacations between stories.

For me, it is the same with books. The only sort of vacation I can really enjoy is a trip to gather more book material. Lying on a beach, or staring at a lake is not for me —unless such a place is going to appear in a story. I find a working vacation so much more interesting than any other.

If your notebook is crammed with story germs, as it should be, you will have several ideas ready to use for your next story before you have this one finished. Then, when your story or book manuscript is in the mail, you dust off your hands and turn *immediately* to the idea that seems best to you and has come to the fore while you were finishing the last story. By writing and finishing another story while one is being considered by an editor, you are building a bulwark against the discouragement of a rejection slip. So what if that story doesn't sell. You send it off again, and now you have another story to send out. Actually, the first thing you know, you may have ten stories making the rounds all at the same time, and that is a wonderful feeling. When one comes back, there are still nine other chances that you may get a check, and, of course, you are adding new ones to those in circulation all the time.

If you want to be a professional writer *quickly,* that is the way to do it. You will not only be getting in the necessary practice to make you perfect, but you will also be getting yourself known among the editors as a producing writer. And editors are not interested in any other kind. They would rather have on call the writer who can repeat with a modest, but workmanlike job several times a year, than the brilliant once-in-five-years variety. Reader following is important.

One of the things which make me want to scream is the writer who says, "Oh, I had a very nice letter from the editor of such-and-such, but somehow I never got around to sending in another story." In case you haven't heard, editors are busy people, too. They certainly don't have time to waste writing to people who take a pat on the back for granted and do nothing more about it. One of the reasons editors use rejection slips rather than letters when returning manuscripts is that they have learned that encouragement to the writers does not necessarily bring in more and better stories.

If an editor takes the time to send you a personal word, no matter how brief, it means that you are being noticed. It means that out of the hundreds of stories pouring over his desk, something in your story stood out sufficiently to appeal to him and make him want to see more. If you let six months go by before you send him another story, you don't deserve to sell it. When you get one of those precious letters from an editor, read that editor's magazine more carefully than ever and try to slant your stories in his direction. Show him you really are serious, even if he sends the next ten stories back to you. Keep at it, and sooner or later, you'll write one that so nearly clicks that he'll be willing to tell you what's the matter with it and give you a chance to revise it. When he buys it, he'll feel an editor's pride in having discovered you.

Of course if you are to achieve this professional attitude toward your work, if you are to reach the place where your output is to be continuous and you turn out story after story, or book after book, with no wasted time in between, then you must have an endless source of material to draw from for ideas. That is a subject for a whole chapter in itself, but first there is something else we must talk about.

5 | TECHNIQUE IS A TOOL

This is where we get down to the serious question of how to do it. The writing of fiction is not an exact science. Each writer must discover for himself his own best method of working. This he does through much experimentation.

Nevertheless, there *are* rules. Or perhaps we can say that some ways of telling a story are more effective than others, if our purpose is to interest and move a reader. Since it is easier to refer to "rules," I have been using this term, but this does not mean that there are laws about writing which *must* govern you and can never be broken.

Certain methods and techniques have proven successful so many times that their use has been accepted by competent writers. A great many published stories disregard one or more of these rules, but that does not mean that it would be wise for you to disregard them in the beginning. Successful writers who are good craftsmen sometimes depart from the rules with a special objective in mind and to achieve some special effect. But you cannot know how a rule may be safely broken until you thoroughly understand the working of that rule.

Don't rely on intuitively and instinctively doing the right thing. *First learn how!* Then if you later choose to break away, you can do it with purpose, not in a haphazard manner that weakens the effect of your story.

But before we consider just what these rules or methods are, it might be well to look at some of the difficulties likely to beset the writer who is learning about technique for the first time. Perhaps you are a person who enjoys the process of writing. When you start a story, you just sit down and write. You haven't worried about technique, or rules, or any such irksome matters. True, your stories haven't been selling, and you would like to remedy that. So you take a correspondence course, enroll in a class, or read a book. You are open-minded—you really do want to learn. You pick up this tool called "technique" and start using it.

The first result is apt to be alarming. You may find that for a time you lose the fluency that was yours before you started learning the rules. You find that instead of showing immediate improvement, your writing has now become stiff and self-conscious. Whatever virtue may have existed in your work vanishes, and you feel that you have gone backwards and are much worse off than you were before.

It is at this point that many novices give up. Somehow, they discover, writing stories is *work,* and it looks much easier than it proves to be. That writing is work is something any *writing* writer knows full well, but that knowledge often comes as a surprise to those who like to sit down to write once in a while.

However, if you really want to write (which may be something altogether different from wanting *to be a writer*), don't let this first awkwardness that is the natural result of trying to learn to handle an unfamiliar tool frighten you off. Acquiring a skill is never simple. From learning to crochet to learning to drive a car, awkwardness comes first, to give way in the end to skill, only *if you persist.* If you stay with it, the rules will become so much a part of you that you can obey them without thinking about them, and the old feeling of fluency will return.

For the writer, technique is a tool with a many-faceted cutting edge. You cannot carve away with one blade and forget about the others. While you are concentrating on characterization, the movement of your story may be slowed. While you labor over your setting, the characterization and plot may be out the window. Somehow you must learn to handle that many-edged tool so that everything is under control at the same time. This is difficult, but with practice it can be done. I know it is useless for me to warn you not to hope to sell what you write during this learning stage. No writer, including me, can sit down at his desk without having the dream of publication, without thinking that surely this story must be *the* one.

But no matter how many times your dream comes to nothing, keep on with the practicing, consciously applying the many edges of your tool to the work in hand. The skill will come.

Can everyone acquire that skill, the skill of writing successful fiction? Of course not. First of all there must be native talent. This should be obvious, but it is surprising how many people with no natural talent at all set out to become writers. Probably because we all are taught from an early age to put words on paper, we are apt to think that is all there is to it. After all, the story in the magazine we picked up last night wasn't so much. Yet that writer got paid for it. So why shouldn't we be paid, too, when we could undoubtedly do better? So our thoughts run.

How do you know whether you have any native talent as a writer? The answer to that question isn't always as easy as it might appear. Of course there are born writers—people who know from the beginning that they *must* write. That simplifies matters a lot. If you're that sort of person, you are eventually going to learn whatever techniques are necessary, and nothing is going to stop you. You may do all the wrong things at first, but despite all the fumbling and blundering and getting off on wrong feet, you'll get there.

However, many people with writing talent don't discover it until they have tried a number of other things first. Fortunately, it is never too late to start to write. You will find successful first books appearing when their authors are thirty-five, or fifty, or even sixty, and have never attempted fiction before in their lives.

I will never forget a talk I had one evening with a man who had published his first novel at sixty-five. He told me regretfully that he knew he would never now have time to say all the things he wanted to say on paper, but that he was happy he had started to write "in time."

Perhaps it is easier for a person of some maturity to begin at the beginning and learn to write, than it is for writers still in their twenties. One of the great handicaps of youth is the dearth of anything significant to say. Until you have lived a while, listened and learned, how can you be worth listening to? So age is an advantage in this regard.

Still, we have not answered that question concerning how you are to know whether or not you have any natural talent for writing. I think it is quite possible that the question cannot be satisfactorily answered. I think it is quite possibly a dangerous question. Certainly, we cannot always judge our own work objectively and fairly. But neither is it always safe to listen to even the most competent critic on this score. Not if he tells you to stop writing. If your work is badly done and full of flaws, it may only mean that at this period in your career, you have not learned enough about the rules. If I had listened to some of the people who advised me in the beginning against going ahead with my writing as I wanted to, I would probably never have sold a story.

Perhaps that is really the way you tell. Whatever the age at which you begin writing, if you refuse to *stay* discouraged, if you retain your ability to bounce back every time you are laid low, if you always find yourself wanting to make one more try—then you are probably going to keep on writing until you succeed. Those who are caught by the glitter and glamour of Being an Author are not able to take it as well, and the drudgery which results in only mediocre efforts will eventually discourage them into giving up.

If you have the writing spark, however early or late it may come to life, are there ways to shorten the road to publication? That question I can answer with a heartfelt, "There are!" And I only wish I'd known that sooner.

True, I mailed out my first story to an editor when I was twenty-one. A very young twenty-one, with nothing of any consequence to say. It was probably necessary that I put a few years behind me just as a matter of seasoning. But even at that, my painful apprenticeship could have been shortened if I had known anything about the shortcuts.

Don't try to start at the top. That is never the way to climb a hill. All my first stories (dozens and dozens of them) were aimed at major national magazines. The rejections which poured in saddened but did not daunt me. I was going to be a writer or else. So I hurled myself at the mountain tops, picked myself up, bruises and all, and tried again. This was a very wearing and silly process, and even I got tired of it after a while. Then I took my eyes off the heights long enough to observe that there were other markets at hand, less glamorous perhaps, but also possibly more within my modest reach. I discovered the newspapers, the pulp paper magazines (long gone now), the church-school publications, and after a still further apprenticeship which did not take as many years, I began to sell regularly to all three.

To try for markets within reach of your capabilities is Recommendation One, and it depends entirely on you. The next recommendation draws in the outside world. If you don't know any other writers, find some. If there isn't a writers' club in your community (this is practically unbelievable), start one. If you can find no more than two other people with the itch to write (this is also fantastic), start with the three of you meeting each week. Read your manuscripts to one another, and tear them apart. No pink-tea-party "isn't it darling!" stuff. Straight-from-the-shoulder criticism, no matter how much it hurts. The criticism may not be too good at first, if yours is a beginners group, but it will help. The purpose of these meetings is mainly to stir you into writing. Competition adds zest. If somebody over on the next block can write a story in no less than a whole month, you ought to be able to do at least as well.

I have heard a lot of harsh and scornful things said about writers' clubs, so I am eager to take this opportunity to speak up for them. "What a waste of time," say the critics. "The way to learn to write is to get busy and start writing. You don't find the real writers going to manuscript-reading fests—they're too busy."

It is true that when you begin selling your work regularly, you will probably be too busy to attend meetings of this sort. Also, many of the "writers" found in these groups are merely hangers-on. It is always nice to say, "I belong to the Pen Pushers, you know." There is no getting away from the fact that the people who want to *be* writers rather than to write clutter up most writers groups.

However, beginning writers need the stimulation that shoptalk with other writers can give them. Professionals can afford to be scornful about this because their own regular appearances in print afford them all the stimulation they need. Beginners do not have this consolation. And what good is learning all about technique if you are not spurred on to the effort that will make you use it?

When I was getting started, I knew no other writers. I

made my first sales without ever exchanging a word with anyone who was bitten by the same bug which I had caught when I was very young. About the nicest thing that happened to me at that time was finding that a new writers group was being formed in Chicago and that I could join it. The fact that I found myself writing harder than ever was proof of how much I needed the kind of stimulation belonging to this group provided. There was nothing so thrilling as to be able to get up in a meeting and be applauded because I had just sold a story for a quarter of a cent a word, instead of being regarded with the well-so-what attitude of those who didn't understand that it wasn't the size of the check that mattered most.

After a time, as the group grew larger, we had professional writers come in to talk to us, and I learned to my astonishment that one didn't necessarily just sit down and write in a hit-or-miss manner. There were actually guidelines; there were better ways than the haphazard methods I was using. I began for the first time to learn about the possible shortcuts I had overlooked all those years.

Somehow you must learn all this. You probably cannot do it effectively alone. There are correspondence courses, there are writing classes, there are books you can read and writers' magazines to subscribe to. You may not immediately burst into print because you are taking some course, or because you have read a book. It will take time to make the things you learn so thoroughly your own that they can work for you.

If you take a course, or enroll in a writing class, try to learn something about the teachers ahead of time. Not all good teachers are necessarily writers, nor is every writer a good teacher. If possible, talk to someone who has taken the course, or sit in on a session before you sign up. Unfortunately, not all teachers of writing are practical, and some of them are not even good critics. You may, without expecting it, find yourself in a Literature Appreciation class, which may not be what you want. A teacher who can help you is priceless. So investigate before you leap.

If you really mean to write, learn as much as you can about craftsmanship. Meet people with whom you can compare notes and talk shop. But don't make the mistake of turning your whole life into a schoolroom. In the final reckoning, the writer is a lone wolf, and just hobnobbing with other writers will not make you a writer. That is something between you and your typewriter.

Suppose at this point we have a look at the so-called rules which govern the writing of a good story. Phases of these rules will be taken up in detail in later chapters, but we need now to take a quick glance at the many edges of this tool called "technique." Some of these rules will apply to any type of writing, but in this case we are interested mainly in applying them to the writing of juvenile fiction.

The following is a checklist of questions you should ask yourself first while your story is in the making, and again when it is completed. Answers to all of these questions should be in the affirmative. When negative answers show up, you will know that that part of your story needs further work and attention.

1. Have you a plot, a story plan?
   a. Is your main character faced by a problem which is very important for him to solve?
   b. Is it a suitable problem for a child of that age?
   c. Is it a problem which will interest other children? (If it is something more likely to interest and please an adult, then it is not suitable for your purpose.)

 d. Are there real obstacles in the path of your main character which prevent him or her from easily achieving his purpose or goal?

 e. Does your main character solve the problem satisfactorily at the end of the story?

2. Is your characterization sound? Are your characters real children whom readers can see and feel they know as individuals? Is the characterization consistent all the way through the story?

3. Does your story have significance? That is, do you have something to say that is important for young people? Does your main character learn and change?

4. Are the various story parts satisfactorily handled?

 a. Does the opening grip the reader's interest immediately?

 b. Does the action in the body of the story continue to be of absorbing interest to readers of the age you are trying to reach?

 c. Does the climax carry a real dramatic punch?

 d. Is the denouement satisfying? Avoid leaving a bad taste. Unpleasant reality may often be included, but the conclusion should point constructively toward hope, if possible, and leave the reader satisfied that the ending is "right" or inevitable.

5. Have you kept to a single viewpoint throughout the story? Does the speech idiom as well as the thought idiom of your viewpoint character ring true all the way through the story?

6. Is your logic sound from beginning to end? If you strain the reader's credulity for the sake of the point you want to make, your story will fail. Just because you, the author, want something to be so, doesn't necessarily mean that it logically is so.

7. Is your dialogue natural?

8. Have you included only such material as is absolutely relevant and necessary to your plot development? Does all action, dialogue, characterization, description, help to move the story toward the climax?

9. Have you avoided the use of trite, hackneyed situations and phrases? Have you avoided the use of clichés?

10. Are your transitions quick and smooth?

11. If you have used flashbacks, are they absolutely necessary? If so, have you handled them clearly so that young readers are not confused and will understand whether your action is taking place in the past or the present?

12. Are your figures of speech suited to the subject and time of the story? Will they seem appropriate to the young readers for whom you are writing?

13. Does the story have emotional value? Does it make your reader feel? (If it doesn't, he might just as well go work a puzzle. The purpose of a story is to convey an emotional experience.)

14. Does the story carry the illusion of reality which makes it really seem to be happening, makes it convincing?

If you can check your story with a "yes" in answer to every one of these questions, the chances are you have a story that will sell.

6 | PERPETUAL MOTION: GETTING STORY IDEAS

This phase of writing can be the most fun. Writers with the habit of observation never lack for material or ideas to write about. A good part of the time, they observe and take mental pictures of what they see, without ever thinking about the process as they do so. The habit of observation and registering impressions mentally becomes as natural to experienced writers as breathing.

Beginners, on the other hand, must observe *consciously.* They must look and listen and wonder how everything they see or hear or experience may be used in a story. Until the habit becomes second nature to them, they are likely to miss a large proportion of the story ideas which are teeming around them. Writers who envy other writers their eye for detail have only to get busy and consciously develop this habit of observation themselves.

They must launch themselves on various idea-collecting projects. They must start files and keep notebooks; they must work out various methods and systems for making themselves aware of what is going on so they will recognize a story idea the second it appears. All this can be fun, a sort of game that is more play than work. Maybe they have a file of pink cards for characters, blue cards for plots, and so on. If a writer sees a small girl he'd like to put into a story, he rushes home to jot the information down in the proper section of the file.

Another writer might have folders for newspaper and magazine clippings, all rich with story ideas, and every day she marks the newspaper carefully, clips selected items and files them under such headings as, "Story Germs," "Hobbies," "Settings," and any others that she thinks may be helpful later on. She may even work out a cross-filing system so that any item can be found at a moment's notice.

This is all just fine and can be extremely profitable. But do it with one eye on that subconscious imp I spoke of earlier. Because he is going to love it. This is no work for him at all and he'll start whispering in your ear, "Isn't this fascinating? Aren't we working hard? Look how professional we're being! All these wonderful things to write about!" And because he kids you into thinking you're being a writer, you may find yourself spending all your time collecting material and *getting ready* to write, instead of actually sitting down and writing (which is the last thing in the world your subconscious wants you to do).

You will certainly need to keep notebooks of ideas, but don't let your system, whatever it is, get too elaborate. Don't forget that the time you spend clipping and filing might very well be better spent at the typewriter *writing*.

The lower drawer in my cabinet always fascinates young writers. It is packed with clippings and pictures of all kinds, neatly arranged under various headings. I keep it as a sort of Exhibit A, but the last date on those clippings runs back over forty years ago. Fortunately, I got too busy writing my ideas into stories to spend time on that file.

At present my "filing" system is pared to the bone. I have a folder headed "Current Work" into which I put various odds and ends pertaining to writing jobs I am working on at the moment. This folder is so actively in use that I keep it on my desk and never put it away in my file.

When I am working on a novel—adult or teen-age—I keep a looseleaf notebook into which I put all the preparatory material concerning the book. This is likely to be too unwieldy to be kept in a folder.

I also keep a smaller notebook on hand which can be tucked into my purse and carried about with me. When I am at home, I keep it near me, whatever I may be doing. Into this I put (in not too tidy fashion) ideas concerning any of my various writing projects. Quite often, when I am writing a review of someone else's book, an apparently unrelated idea will pop into my mind that may apply to my own book. I jot this down quickly, before it is lost. Such ideas can come to me anywhere, any time—when I am riding on a train, waiting in a dentist's office, or shopping for groceries. If I wait to write it down later, I know I'll probably forget—hence, the ever-present notebook.

Since I no longer write short stories, I have dispensed with the casual note-taking which the short story writer must do. Because each of my projects takes a number of months to complete, I make my notes and collect material with a specific, definite purpose in mind, and as little wasted motion as possible.

But if you are just breaking into writing for publication, I hope you plan to write short stories first. Even if you eventually find, as I did, that you are better suited by temperament to writing books, I would suggest that you spend an apprenticeship in short story writing, before you attempt a book. Working with the shorter length will condition you so thoroughly to telling a story and keeping it moving that when you do start to write a book this habit and discipline will be well established and will carry over to the longer form. When I pick up a book for young people and find it slow and rambling, lacking in pace, not getting anywhere fast enough, I know the writer has not had this much-needed training in the short story field. It is much easier to write a book than it is to write a short story. Therefore, if you learn the more difficult form first, you will be forever after grateful for the things it will teach you. To this day, even in writing a long (400-page) novel, I write sparely and seldom cut. The first draft runs closer to three hundred pages, but I expand and write in extra scenes—something that is easier for me than having to cut.

In writing a short story for young people, you learn first not to allow reader interest to let up at any point. Being forced to put your story into the confines of a really difficult wordage limit (say two thousand words), you learn to free yourself of any clutter of descriptive material, or of detail unnecessary to your single purpose of making that story move ahead.

I learned that the end of a scene in a story can be a danger point. Before there is even a slight slowing of interest on the part of young readers, throw in some new matter, connected directly, of course, with the main story problem, but raising some new problems for your hero. You must not fail to rouse in your readers' minds a question they cannot bear to let go unanswered. A story which draws a reader's interest on from scene to scene by such a method inevitably has pace. It moves, and there is always something interesting happening.

Having learned this rule in writing short stories for young people, I did not need to relearn it in writing a book. It was something I continued to apply to my longer stories. As a consequence, reader interest is sustained from first to last chapter, and there is no danger (whatever other faults the books have) of having readers put aside my books in boredom because the writer "doesn't get to the story." It is amazing how long some book writers take to get to their stories, and I cannot help but feel that if they had gone through a rigorous training period in the shorter form, they would write much more interesting books.

My system of note-taking (now pared down) when I was writing short stories consisted of my keeping four notebooks. One was the usual hard-working purse size; two were medium-size loose-leaf notebooks; the fourth was a small loose-leaf. One of the middle-sized notebooks I kept faithfully as a plot book; it served as one of my most important sources of story ideas. The second took a lot of time to keep up, but I am glad I did so for a number of years, because it is still useful to me in many ways. I read always with a pencil in hand, and when I came across a passage in some book or story which struck me as unusually significant, I would copy it into my notebook. In it are paragraphs from books by Thomas Mann, Somerset Maugham, Rebecca West, and a great many others. In it, too, are pertinent passages from the autobiographies of various writers—Arnold Bennett, Edna Ferber, Gamaliel Bradford. Included as well are sections from various books on psychology.

Into your purse-size notebook you will write anything that appeals to you at the moment it comes to mind. You can think of most of this as plot-germ material, and later type it into the plot notebook.

The fourth book is an alphabetical listing of names. First names and last names, foreign names, names for boys and for girls. To make a collection of that kind is simple enough, takes practically no time, and can save you much thinking and searching when you want to name a character. You can start such a book simply by jotting down all the names you can think of. After that you collect names from every book or story you read, or any unusual name you may hear. Now I use a name-the-baby book as an extra help.

So much for what you do with your ideas, once you have them. Now for that well-worn question: "Where do you get your ideas?"

Everywhere, of course, is the answer, but let's be a bit more specific. Once you have developed that "seeing eye," you'll collect ideas continuously. By way of an experiment, try this the next time you walk through a department store. You were probably intent on your purchases, but now suppose you retrace your steps looking for story material. It is amazing how the color and bustle of that store will suddenly come alive for you and be a thousand times more interesting than it was when you walked down the same aisle a few minutes before, not consciously looking for story ideas.

The clerks behind the counters are characters now. So are the customers. The entire scene is rich with atmosphere and plot material. But remember—you're going to write for children, so you have to look at this from the angle of your young reader. What would attract a small boy on this aisle? A small girl? Or a teen-ager?

Do you really know, or are you just guessing? I can think of no better way for a writer to find out what attracts children than to take a group of youngsters of varying ages on a shopping tour and give them free rein. You may spend the next day in bed, but you'll be led in unexpected directions and you'll learn a lot.

Sensory perception is of primary importance to the young child. He reacts keenly to color and size and shape, to sound and smell, and very strongly to touch. Upon seeing some object for the first time, the immediate impulse of the young child is to reach out to touch it. Having made its acquaintance through eager fingertips, having found whether it is smooth or rough, hot or cold, soft or hard, he is then prepared to take it into the ever-expanding boundaries of his world and give it a recognizable place. It is this desire to touch that has led to books in which actual materials are used to give the small child the experience of touching various surfaces and textures.

But these devices are mere gimmicks. Writers have available for their use figures of speech which will link the new to what the child already knows, and so they are not bound only to the sense of touch. What is more, writers who are wise enough to use sensory perception to the fullest degree in their stories will bring to the scenes they describe that illusion of reality without which any story falls flat.

One of the most useful purposes to be served by books for children is to introduce young readers to new experiences they might not have in the course of their everyday living, and thus broaden their horizons. This can be achieved in great part by learning what sensory details attract children of different ages and using this knowledge fully in one's writing.

Stir up your imagination and see what you come up with. You may find it a little sluggish and slow to respond at first, but with prodding, you will keep it constantly at work for you.

Wherever you go, collect sounds and odors, and the feel, even the taste, of things. And I don't mean only the taste of food. Dry, dusty air has a taste. So has fresh, salty sea air, or sunny country air, or air heavy with fog. In touching objects, think about how they feel. Are they warm or cold? Do they feel limp or hard, rough or smooth? What other familiar objects do these things resemble? Don't rely only on your fingers for touch sensation. How does snow feel against your face? Or water against your body? How does that inviting pillow feel behind your back?

If you make a habit of collecting details of this kind using all of your senses, you will find your writing enriched and

enlivened far beyond the effort it will take. Children especially are lovers of detail, and they will prize your stories if
you can bring alive in words their everyday world, as well
as some new world to which your story introduces them.
In letter after letter over the years, children have written
me that they feel they are there in my stories while they are
reading. They live the experience. And that is what we
want to give our readers in fiction.

Of course your main source of idea material will be your
own past experiences. "Write about what you know" is advice given so often to young writers that they are apt to
cringe at hearing it one more time. For some curious reason young writers seldom want to write about what they
know. Not having as yet developed that "seeing eye" which
recognizes story material everywhere, these writers feel that
only the things they know nothing whatsoever about are interesting. I went through this foolish state—I know what
it's like.

I spent the first fifteen years of my life in the Orient. I
had the most vivid memories of China and Japan and the
Philippine Islands. But while other young writers I knew
were trying to sell stories about a Shanghai they had never
seen, I was bent on writing about Hollywood night clubs—
which I had never seen. To me the Orient was everyday
stuff and not half so exciting as America. When I got out
of school, I worked for several years selling books in department stores. Nothing seemed more tiresome to me, and I
went home at night to spend my writing hour describing
the lives of people I knew nothing about.

One of the quickest ways to start getting what you write
accepted and published is to recognize the rich ore right in
your own backyard, however prosaic it may look to you.
After a while, I woke up and began to write stories of American children in the Orient for church-school papers, and

they sold because I knew what I was talking about. Years later, when I was no longer working in a department store selling books, I began to see the glamorous and fascinating aspects of book-selling as a career: I wrote *A Star for Ginny* (my second book), which is about a girl working at her first job in the book section of a department store. In fact, my experience working in a department store eventually led to my writing three books with that setting and background.

In time, however, you may reach the stage when you have exhausted that backyard material. You may go into a discouraging slump and feel completely dried up when it comes to story ideas. Your notebooks and files net you nothing but yawns, and you suffer the painful frustration of a writer who wants to write but who has nothing to say. This is serious, and it is likely to come at one time or another to every writer. Sometimes this only means that you are in a transition period and are now ready for the next step up. You may be writing yourself out of your old markets and yet be unwilling to relinquish them completely before you are sure of yourself in a new field. Or it may mean that you really have used up the stock of material in your memory storehouse and have neglected to fill those empty shelves with fresh goods.

In either case, the treatment is not to sit around at home while you wait for a story idea to come in and bite you. The thing to do at that point is to go out and bite a few story ideas!

I came out of my worst slump with a rule which has been so useful to me that I have never since that time run out of ideas. It is just this: *Interest follows action.* First, you *do* something—then you get interested. So many people think it should be the other way around and that you have to be interested before you care about doing anything. This, of course, gets you nowhere.

Following this rule, you can pull yourself out of any slump by picking a subject out of the air. It makes not the slightest difference whether you have any interest in it or not. When you start doing something about it the interest will come and the door will open that will lead somewhere.

The first time I applied this rule, the subject I picked was "department store advertising." Probably it came to mind because at the conclusion of *A Star for Ginny* my heroine was going into the advertising department to work as an artist. As a matter of fact, I remember finishing the book with a feeling of relief, because *I* knew nothing about the career she meant to enter, and I certainly couldn't write about it at that point.

At any rate, that was the dry-as-dust (as far as I was concerned) subject to which I decided to apply my interest-follows-action rule. Regardless of my apathy toward the subject, I decided to force myself out of my comfortable armchair and into the field. Bored as I was at the prospect, I was determined to find out something about department store advertising at first hand.

The exciting thing about this sort of adventurous undertaking (and it certainly is that) is that you never know where you'll end up. The chances are you will branch off down some fascinating side road leading to undreamed-of shores. I did not write a book about department store advertising; I still know little about the subject, but that was my springboard. It started me off on a quest that brought me as rich a collection of new experiences and new material to write about as I could have hoped to find.

Do you know how a sponge feels? You should try to figure it out, because you need to make yourself into a sort of animated sponge when you start the action which is going to create interest in your apathetic soul. You must soak up everything that comes along; you can reject nothing. Through every pore, you will absorb material until that moment when you feel as if an electric switch is thrown and brings interest to life in you for weeks and months to come.

The first step is the hardest to take because of your inertia. It is so much easier to drift along and make no effort to stand up and push yourself into action. The first push I gave myself was toward an appointment with a young woman who wrote advertising in a department store. I went to see her, not too hopefully, but armed with a notebook.

Her office was a cubbyhole, and she was terribly busy. I sat in a corner and waited. As I waited, things began to seep in through my sponge pores, whether I invited them or not. To begin with, this wasn't the sort of office I'd ever seen before. It could have been very drab and ugly, but its pretty, smart-looking occupant had covered all the wall space from floor to ceiling with pages torn from various magazines. There were fascinating color photographs, interesting black-and-whites, stunning advertisements. I could never have dreamed up that room sitting at home. I had to go out and expose myself to it. Even in my lackluster state, I determined that if I could ever again think of a story I would have to put that office into it. Eventually the office went into not one, but two full-length books.

As I sat there, things kept happening. People popped in and out, chattering about their various store problems. It was all very informal, and nobody paid any attention to me. I didn't know it, but somewhere in my subconscious a hand was moving stealthily toward that electric switch.

When the person I had come to see had time to talk to me, I told her I was planning to write a career book for girls about department store advertising and would she tell me a little about her job. The wonderful part about approaching story ideas in this manner is that you never know what is around the next corner, or how suddenly you may be plunged into an Alice-in-Wonderland world.

My chosen career woman began to talk obligingly enough about her job, and I found that she didn't write the sort of advertising I'd had vaguely in mind. She wrote copy for all the sign cards that were used throughout the store and in the windows. Writing sign copy, it seemed, was quite an art. You not only wrote it, you designed the card itself in some cases, indicating the materials which would make it up, and the colors which were to be used. The colors, of course, had to fit in with the display to be shown in the window.

"You ought to go to see our window display department," she said. "I should think that would be an awfully interesting place for a writer."

The hand reached the switch and on went a blinding light where there had been only darkness for months past. It was all settled in an instant. I was going to write a vocational novel for girls about window decorating, and I knew without a doubt that I was going to have the time of my life finding out all about the subject. What was more, I was going to be exposed to a whole rash of story ideas.

It wasn't always easy. I had to pull more than one string, and be very persistent before I wangled my way behind the scenes into a window-display department. Very little had been written on the subject, and I found I had to get nearly all my material firsthand. The assistant display manager at one store took an interest in what I wanted to do and let me trail around after him, notebook in hand, taking down everything I saw and heard, asking foolish questions, soaking up atmosphere.

He was particularly interested in showing me one big room in the department which was lined all the way around with cabinets. In these cabinets were arms, legs, heads, torsos and all the various parts of window mannequins. Another light clicked on in my mind, and I thought, "What a wonderful place for a murder." By the time I went home that day, I knew that I was still going to write a book for girls about window decorating, but before I did that I was going to write a murder mystery for adults using exactly the same background.

Out of that experience, out of going out and exposing myself to story ideas, came the two books: *Red Is for Murder* and *A Window for Julie*. By the time I finished them, I could practically qualify as a window decorator myself. It was work—I had to spend hours on the scene, collecting material. I stood outside many a window display writing down things I had never noticed before in my casual shopping tours. But out of reality came story material in richly rewarding quantities. One of the notes I made had to do with a large spray gun I noticed among the odds and ends of the display department. I asked if they were bothered with flies and was told that the gun contained a pine substance that had been sprayed around the store at Christmas time. I had no idea what I could do with a pine spray, but I wrote it down in my notebook. Later it helped to solve my mystery story. And a pair of fascinating pink horses used in a baby window display so intrigued me that I worked them into the climax of my girls' book.

Red Is for Murder didn't do well in the beginning: It earned all of $640 for six months' work and went out of print in 1948. Seventeen years later the Gothic craze hit, and I found I was a Gothic writer. So *Red Is for Murder* was reissued in paper as *The Red Carnelian*—and it is still doing very well. You never know what may happen to those good ideas. (*A Window for Julie* has been long out of print.)

I have told about this experience in detail because I feel that this system is one of the best you can possibly use to stimulate the imagination and get yourself launched on more story ideas than you can write in a lifetime. It takes a lot of effort, but never too much. Such material, once stored away in notebooks and memory, can serve you endlessly from that time on. Nothing is ever wasted.

One of the special virtues of getting story material in this fashion is that it is likely to give your story that "different" touch which may appeal to an editor. Editorial desks are swamped with stories about the same old stuff. Old stuff is good if handled in a fresh new way, or if some of the story elements are so outstanding that they make the story irresistible. But if you are just breaking in and want to attract attention, the quickest way to do it is by getting something novel and unusual into your story.

In a lifetime of writing, I have developed this very system I used for my early books into something that keeps me writing, even though it would seem that I would long ago have run out of story material. Now I look for background first, whether it be a foreign country, or a locality nearer home but with which I am unacquainted. I do research in the library, visit the place, soak myself in "atmosphere," and then come home to write both a romantic suspense novel (which name I prefer to "Gothic") and a teen-age mystery using the same locale. All that early training has paid off handsomely.

Concerning the use of "real" places, situations and people as the source of your story material, I'd like to make a point. Sooner or later every book reviewer or editor who has condemned a book or manuscript has had the writer counter with the protest, "But it really happened." I hope you will never be guilty of using that old defense. That the events in your story "really happened" doesn't mean a thing. Very often what really happens does not make good story material because it is much too coincidental and far-fetched to be believed as fiction. The point is not whether something happened, but whether you can make the reader *believe* it happened. So while you are collecting your material, remember that in the final reckoning it must be blended into fiction. Your story may have a firm grounding in reality, but it will be an interpretation of reality, rather than life itself.

7 | THREE NECESSARY INGREDIENTS: EMOTION, SIGNIFICANCE, IMMEDIACY

The best definition I know of a short story is one which Frederic Nelson Litten gave to his fiction writing classes at Northwestern University many years ago: "A short story is a narrative with an emotional purpose."

Intellectual pyrotechnics on paper seldom make the sort of writing that lasts. If you look back to those stories and books you have remembered over the years, you will find that in every case they gave you an *emotional experience*. Whether the emotion was one of delight, elation, pity, anger, disgust—or whatever—in reading that story or book you were made to *feel*.

It is in this area particularly that the beginner's manuscript falls flat. The reader, putting the story down, feels nothing at all. His major reaction is "so what?" This is far too often true of stories for children, even of some which get published. Perhaps the writers have been so long out of touch with the things about which children feel strongly that they are no longer able to capture such emotion on paper and transfer it to a reader.

How does the writer convey emotion? It is possible to feel strongly while writing and still not get that feeling down on paper. There are techniques for accomplishing this, as there are for everything else in writing.

One important step is to watch the *reaction* of your characters. How do they respond to what happens in each scene? In that response lies emotion. Any sort of response grows out of feeling, large or small. Omit it so that the character appears to feel nothing, and the reader will feel nothing either. What is in *your* mind isn't enough. It must be down there on paper.

Here are some examples from my *Secret of Haunted Mesa:*

> "Please come in," she said to Jenny. "I want you to tell me about the yellow smock with the penny in the pocket."
>
> For an instant Jenny could not move. But the door was open and the woman stood waiting. Feeling a little frightened now, Jenny obeyed the command of that waiting figure.

It isn't always necessary to name the emotion, but we need to understand it. Here is a passage that comes a little later in the story:

> This was the strangest conversation she had ever had, Jenny thought. It was as though this woman, who had lived a very long time, and Jenny Hanford, who had lived comparatively few years, had made some sort of bridge between them, where neither was young or old. They were just two people who could talk to each other. Perhaps it was because neither knew the other well and didn't expect certain things of the other person. Jenny found that she was mildly curious about what would happen next in this strange situation, but she no longer felt any anxiety, no longer felt apologetic.

Here is a passage toward the climax of the story:

> "The Shalako has begun," Consuelo Eliot whispered. "For him it is winter and he is not alone."
>
> Jenny's skin prickled at the words. She could see what was meant. It was as if that single dancer out there on the mesa top moved in concerted steps with many others. By his gestures and movements he recognized other dancers . . .

Jenny could almost see a hundred people out there—watching, like themselves.

Naturally, without the build-up of all that has gone before—since all aspects of a story should build toward emotion—the feeling cannot be conveyed in excerpted passages. However, in each of these examples, we know what the main character is feeling, through her thoughts, her *reactions*.

When action is very exciting and dramatic, it isn't always necessary to stop for the main character to think and react. That can come later during a "rest" scene. What is happening should in itself carry an emotional punch if you have built well. However, when the feeling or emotion is more subtle, it is necessary to show it in the reaction of the main character to it, and we also want to know what other characters are feeling. But this can't be done through their thoughts unless you break viewpoint—which is not advisable. Instead of shifting viewpoint, you must describe actions or expressions of those other characters so that the main character can see and interpret them. The reaction of your main character must also be shown.

In his book, *Writing Non-Fiction,* Walter S. Campbell made a point well worth consideration by fiction writers:

> Men differ greatly in their thoughts, far less in their emotions, and hardly at all in their sensations.

If you want to put across a thought (an idea, a moral) in your story, don't begin with that. Before you can reach your reader and make him come over to your side in his beliefs, you must reach him through his emotions. You must make him *feel*. In order to make him feel, let him experience a sensation or emotion in common with one of the characters. If you as a writer can make the reader identify himself or herself with an emotion felt by that character, then what is painful, for example, to that character becomes painful to the reader.

If you are going to touch the emotions of your readers, if you are going to make them feel deeply, if you are going to make them care about your story people, care what happens, you must understand first of all what your readers want of life. And you must be sympathetic toward those wants. There is a universality about human needs, no matter what the age or position of the people involved. When you understand that, there will be no danger of your writing down to the readers, and your stories will take on a warmth that will make your readers respond with genuine feeling.

Anyone who knows the children's book field will tell you that a good story for children should be enjoyable to readers of any age. It should not, for example, bore the mother who is reading it aloud, even though it is only the short text contained in a picture book.

Tom Sawyer, Treasure Island, Heidi, The Secret Garden —any book you mention that has lived through the years— can be read and enjoyed by anyone. These books have the quality of universality because the authors understood human beings.

What your readers want of life is not so very different from what you want. They want affection, to be approved of, to have a sense of worth in the scheme of things. They want to feel that there are "adventures" to be met, even in the course of everyday living. And so you write stories about someone like your reader. You prove that there are adventures to be found around almost every corner. You show how the character in the story got off on the wrong foot and people didn't like him very much. He then learns how to win approval, but in a pleasant way.

When you are writing for older children, your task is exactly the same. That teen-age girl who will be your reader wants other young people to like her. She wants to straighten out school problems, boy problems, job problems. She wants to feel that life doesn't have to be a dull, repetitious routine forever and forever. So in your story you help straighten out these things: You help her over the rough spots that are sure to come, and you help her to understand the good old rule about life being what you make it. If you can't sympathize with what your readers want of life, if you cannot look upon people of all sorts and all ages with generosity and compassion, then you have no business trying to be a writer.

Often young readers write me to say: "That's *my* problem. That's how it is in *my* family. I felt good because the character in your story worked it out."

Perhaps this is part of what fiction can do for any reader. It can show that no one of us is alone or unique, that others have been over this road, too, and found a way. Or if the character gave up and wasn't able to cope, readers can see that, too, and perhaps it is useful to understand why.

Significance and emotion are tied together closely. If you want your reader to feel emotion while he is reading your story, you must have something worthwhile to say. Most stories which have something to say will be found to have a theme. It is a good idea to set down in a single sentence just what you want to say in your story. Sometimes when you analyze old stories you have written (the ones that didn't sell), you will find that you were trying to say at least six different things in 2,500 words. Better pick one main thread and hew to it all the way through. In a book, you may have a major theme and several minor contributing themes, but in the space of a short story you had better confine yourself to one clear idea or theme.

Here are a few themes I have used in short stories:

1. Under the superficial differences all people are the same.

2. A popular girl who is always sure of herself and runs other people's lives with a high hand may need to learn that she, too, can be mistaken.

3. A sacrifice made for another may bring the giver a rich reward.

I suggest that you start jotting your own themes down in that plot notebook. A theme is anybody's property and may be used over and over again in stories that will bear no resemblance to other stories written around the same theme. The Bible is of course filled with themes. Any book of proverbs will net you hundreds. It is a profitable idea to analyze every story you read for its underlying theme and add that theme to your collection. To be effective, of course, it must be something *you* believe.

If you work a theme into your story and handle it well, you can be sure that story will have significance. Editors in the children's field are always looking for writers who have something worth saying. Today, they call it "relevance." Also, a theme will help give your story a single effect. Without a theme, your story parts may be scattered loosely in an unconnected fashion, like unstrung beads. The theme is the thread that gathers all your beads into one firm strand that begins at a set point and ends at a set point.

The third necessary ingredient in your story is immediacy. That means that you must give your reader the feeling that something is happening *now*. Blocks of information are sure interest-killers. In order to test your writing for this element, it is a good idea to consider your story as a play. Then ask yourself if the scene is being performed before your eyes, or if a narrator has stepped out in front of the curtain to talk about the play. Away with narrators!

No one has time to listen to them these days. Give us action, give us something happening *right now*.

Here are examples of the wrong and the right way to handle a scene:

> Julie went up to the display department to get the stork and take it down to the window. But when she reached the department she found that the bracket which had held the stork was empty. This disturbed her very much, but she thought one of the helpers must have carried it downstairs. Finally she walked across the room and discovered with horror that the stork had fallen to the floor and been broken to bits.

In that version somebody is telling us about it; we are not living the scene through Julie. Now, let's raise the curtain on the play and see how it looks when the same scene was presented with immediacy in *A Window for Julie*.

> There were no lights burning in the department, and for a moment Julie thought she heard someone moving in one of the rooms.
>
> "Hello!" she called. "Who's there?"
>
> But there was no answer and the sound of her own voice echoing through emptiness had a startling effect on her nerves. Gracious, she thought, was she going to start believing in ghosts at this late date? A window display department would certainly make a wonderful place to haunt! She chuckled at her foolish thoughts and hurried to the door of the workroom. It was dark and she had to fumble a moment for the light. Her fingers found the switch, turned it, and the room sprang into life in all its familiar aspects. But Julie stood in the doorway in startled dismay, scarcely believing the evidence of her own eyes.
>
> The bracket which held the stork was empty.
>
> There could be only one explanation, of course. One of the helpers had come up for it on his own, not knowing that

she meant to carry it down herself. Probably it was already in the window by now and Bill was busy hanging it.

That was what she wanted to believe, but something held her there in the doorway. Then, almost as if she moved against her will, she stepped quietly into the room, walked around Kim's worktable, and stood staring in horror. What remained of her precious stork lay shattered at her feet.

The first example is mere summary. The second gives the scene in detail as it happens, and if we have followed the story up to that point, we can experience the same shock of horror Julie feels.

At times when it is necessary to get over unimportant happenings in a hurry, you may need to summarize. But never summarize your important scenes—show them happening. And remember that even necessary summary is deadening to reader interest, so don't clutter up your story with it.

Before we leave the subject, I'd like to make a further point concerning the tremendously important factor of emotion. While you can understand why the second version of this scene is more effective than the first, I am sure that you did not feel any particular emotion in reading the scene. That is because you had not read what went before. You could not know how much depended upon that stork as far as Julie was concerned. Emotion is an element which is built up in a story from the first paragraph. It is built up through liking and sympathy for the character, through understanding of the problem that faces her, and a perception of how much depends on her success.

To sum up: *Make your reader feel. Have something to say. Show it happening now.*

8 | CHARACTERIZATION

I have known writers to carry on endless controversies concerning the primary importance of (a) characterization, and (b) plot. One group claims that the plot is of no consequence and will grow naturally enough out of character action, once you get your characters worked out so they can take over. *Character* Is All-Important. The second group claims that plot is of first importance, and until you know what sort of story you are going to tell, you can't even know what types of characters you'll need to use. *Plot* Is All-Important.

When the argument becomes really heated, the first group uses the scornful term "commercial" to describe the second, and the second group counters with scathing remarks about "art-for-art's sake." And nobody gets anywhere.

In my opinion (and I realize that both groups will probably jump on me), plot and characterization are inextricably bound together. To discuss which comes first is as futile as to argue the old chicken-or-the-egg controversy. I am taking characterization first, not because I consider it of primary importance—I don't; I consider it of *equal* importance—but because I have to start somewhere.

If you are having difficulty in getting emotion into your stories, some of the trouble may come from poor characterization. Obviously, without understanding, sympathy,

73

insight into a child's nature, no writer for children can get
very far. But starting from that basis of understanding, the
next requirement is knowing what tools to use for characterization; and when you have learned what they are, you
must next learn by consistent practice how to use them
effectively. Finally, you will need a measuring stick to test
each story when it is completed.

Long before you reach the point of putting words on paper, you decide certain things about your fictional people.
You choose first of all a viewpoint character. If you are
writing for children, do, please, make your viewpoint character a child. It is amazing how often writers starting out in
this field will pick an adult for a viewpoint character—
someone whose problems and interests are not a child's problems and interests. Your young reader wants to see your
story through young eyes like his own. If you happen to be
writing an animal story in which you cannot write from the
viewpoint of a child, then see that your main character is a
young animal. I cannot plead too often with the writer of
children's stories to use children for characters and keep
adults to a role of minimum necessity. There are already
too many interfering grownups in the life of any young
person.

Breaking this very rule, however, I have sometimes used
adult characters to good effect in my books for young people. The viewpoint character is always young, but sometimes an interesting older person plays an important role.
In *Secret of the Haunted Mesa,* the woman, Consuelo Eliot
and the young girl who is the main character become good
and understanding friends, reaching across the generations
to learn from each other. Young Jenny is given a glimpse of
adult suffering and courage that comforts her in her own
life and helps her to grow. And Jenny draws Consuelo away
from her rejection of life. Consuelo is in herself un-

usual and interesting, and she seems to appeal to my readers. The story is, of course, kept on the level of Jenny's interests and problems. The scenes between the young person and the old are suspenseful, and sometimes there is conflict—all of which helps to build interest.

In a book called *Mystery of the Angry Idol,* I used an old woman who is the main character's grandmother, and in *Mystery of the Hidden Hand* there is a grandfather who is an interesting and likable character. So it can work, but in the main, young people want to read about others their own age; adults should appear only when necessary to a scene.

If you want your story to carry an emotional impact, it is wise to select one character and tell the story from his viewpoint from beginning to end. Otherwise, you will be jumping around from the emotional outlook of one child to another, and the effect will be confusion for the reader. If you write from a single viewpoint, you will present nothing that character cannot see and hear and feel and smell. You will present no thoughts which are not thoughts of the viewpoint character, unless they are given through spoken words and he or she is on the spot to hear them. No matter how exciting a scene going on in the next room may be, unless you can devise a logical means for getting Johnny or Jane into that room, don't try to present that scene in your story.

So many writers break this elementary rule that it cannot be emphasized too often. If your viewpoint skips from character to character throughout the story, you scatter your shots, weaken the emotional effect. And every time you switch viewpoints, you cause an inevitable letdown in story interest.

Not only do beginners break the rule of single viewpoint in their manuscripts, but in book after published book which comes my way it is obvious that the writers never heard of—or certainly do not observe—that rule, and what is worse, the editor has let them get away with doing so. Sometimes this is called the "omniscient" viewpoint, but that term lends dignity to a practice which I refuse to endorse. Rarely, as a matter of fact, does this vague, all-over-the-place viewpoint help a story.

Near the beginning of this book, I said there were no absolute rules for writing. The advice to write from a single viewpoint, however, is as close to being an absolute rule as any. At least you should train yourself in the habit of using the single point of view until you can handle it well and appreciate its advantages. When you have accomplished that, you many never want to write any other way. Or if you decide later to break the rule, you will know why you are doing so and how to do it. You will not have fallen into a bad habit because you did not know any better.

In a full-length book, viewpoint may be changed to various characters if you retain the single viewpoint throughout each chapter. *Don't* shift viewpoint several times in one chapter, and above all, don't shift it several times on one page. If you are writing a short story, you'll do a much more workmanlike job if you retain the single viewpoint straight through the story.

The first-person story is, of course, the perfect example of single viewpoint writing. It is very easy to hold to one viewpoint when the leading character is "I." But first-person writing is not always popular with young readers and is therefore frowned upon by editors except in some especially good stories. Every librarian has had the experience of hearing some child say, "But I don't like 'I' books!"

Though I may have softened my feeling about the first-person viewpoint over the years, and perhaps things have changed a bit, I have recently found that a certain young character I was working on seemed to want to talk in the first person. So I let her do as she wished, and I can't see that these first-person books have been any less popular than my third-person stories. In the adult field, I find there is a sense of immediacy to the first person that lends itself to a building of suspense. So when it appeals to me, I shall probably use this form from time to time in children's books as well.

It is more difficult to retain the single viewpoint when you are writing in the third person. If you are having trouble mastering this, it is good practice for you to write the story in the first person just to get the feeling of it. Then, once you have it down on paper, you can change the story into third person.

If you are uncertain as to which of your characters to choose as the point-of-view character, select the one to whom the most trouble is likely to happen. Conflict, trouble, disaster, all mean story interest, and it is much better to tell the story from the viewpoint of the character who will be most active.

At any rate, you must identify yourself thoroughly with your viewpoint character. You must not only keep to the idiom of speech he would use in speaking, but you must also keep to the idiom of his thought, which is most difficult of all.

If you are writing from the viewpoint of a child who is watching his or her mother across the room, don't have the character think: "Mother seemed preoccupied that evening." "Preoccupied" is a natural enough word for you to use, but it is not in the idiom of the child about whom you are writing, and if you are to stay in the shoes, in the skin, in the mind of that child, you will be more likely to write: "Mother seemed awfully quiet that evening." In order to heighten the emotional effect which is the primary purpose of your story, you want the reader to identify with your viewpoint character. You cannot do this successfully if you keep skipping out of character and sounding like some older person.

When you have decided on your viewpoint character, give her or him a name and identity. Who is this girl or boy? How old? Describe his or her appearance. This description will be mainly for your own edification, since you won't have room for it in detail in the space of a short story. But that appearance should be clear in your own mind. If Johnny has red freckles on his nose and is sturdily built, see him that way. If Mary has blue eyes and an elfin look about her, get her appearance set in your own imagination. But don't fancy just because you can now see your characters that they are real people. Chances are you still have only a name, an outward shell, perhaps a type. You may have a poor little rich girl, a poor but honest farm boy, a teacher's pet, or a teacher's pest, or any of the hundreds of other categories into which we can pigeonhole characters, young and old. Which is all right. It will help you to see your characters to get them typed. But you won't have people until you individualize within the type.

Living children are made up of so many traits that it would be impossible, even in a novel, to portray one in the full dimensions of life. Not even Tom Sawyer is done as completely as that. It is the writer's task to select such characteristics as will be useful in telling the story. In the case of your main character, one important character trait may be chosen, along with two or three lesser traits. If some of these are slightly contradictory, all the better: your character will be more apt to resemble an individual child.

I am asked sometimes if I use real people for my characters. As it happens, I do not. Real people get in my way. If I try to write about a girl I know named Mary Jones, I am likely to find before I am very far into the story that the Mary I know is proving obstinate. Because my characters and plot are so thoroughly interwoven, I come to a place where, for the sake of the story I want to tell, Mary would have to do or say something which the real Mary would never do or say. And the planning process is hindered. So it is better if my Mary is a composite of many girls I know. Then she can be the kind of person I need for this particular story without in the least flying in the face of reality.

In the case of your viewpoint character, you will have one major advantage and one major disadvantage. You will be able to characterize him through his own thoughts, and you will be able to characterize all your other characters by looking at them through his eyes and thinking about them with his mind. This is all to the good. As a disadvantage you will not be able to look at your viewpoint character through outside eyes and you cannot tell what other characters are thinking about him unless they choose to express themselves in word or by action.

Another difficulty which occurs in the single viewpoint story, whether third or first person is used, is in describing the main character. Your reader will want to know something of that character's appearance; yet you can't always stand Mary and John in front of a mirror and have them describe the image they see reflected there. That's been done too many times, and sometimes I still do it! In using third person, you often begin objectively, showing the reader what the main character looks like, and then zeroing in to get inside.

This can't be done if you're using first person, in which you must be inside from the very beginning. However, your heroine (or hero) knows how she looks, and various more subtle ways than a mirror can be devised to convey this information to the reader. For example:

She looked down at her tanned hands folded on the knees of her blue jeans. . .

She faced the angry blue intensity of her mother's eyes—so very like her own. . .

I knew I'd never grow as big as my father. Lots of people call me a shrimp. . .

Brown eyes run in my family, but I've always wished I had big blue ones like my friend Joan. . .

And so on and on. In the stories and books you read, see how it is done. Becoming a writer also makes you a critic, and it's a good idea to recognize clumsiness as well as skill in other writers. *You* can always try to do better.

Through the eyes of your viewpoint character, you will set the scene, give his reactions to that scene, further the action of the story, and accomplish many other purposes. For example:

With the sight of the house her spirits took a sudden upward zoom and she knew at once why the Tarrants endured the neighborhood. The structure was more queer than beautiful, perhaps, but it stood out as a real personality among its uninteresting neighbors. It reminded Ginny of an illustration for a fairy tale and she longed for a pencil and sketch block.

This paragraph characterizes both the neighborhood and the girl, and it moves her toward her destination—the house.

Perhaps you are still not altogether willing to concede that you can tell a better story by using a single viewpoint. Perhaps you have been jumping happily around from character to character in your stories and resent having someone rap your knuckles and tell you not to do it any more. All right—let's have a look at a few paragraphs of writing in which the viewpoints are mixed.

Bill glowered at his oatmeal. Ordinarily the stuff was okay, but not when it rained on Saturday. On a rainy Saturday nothing would taste good. The gang had been going to get together and practice football plays in the yard that was now being stirred into a big mud pie. Tony Bryan, one of the boys from high school had promised to come over and give them all pointers. But now . . .

Across the table Bill's sister Sally was scraping the bottom of her bowl. Rainy Saturdays were wonderful. Mother had promised that on the very next Saturday it rained she could go up and spend the morning looking through grandmother's trunk in the attic. There would be wonderful dress-up things in that trunk. It was too bad Bill was looking so cross, though. Probably he wouldn't care about the trunk. But how Bill felt didn't matter. She smiled happily to herself, looking very pretty with her big blue eyes dancing and her lips wearing a sunny smile.

Mrs. Hall regarded her two children with mixed emotions. Bill was getting to be more and more of a problem lately, turning sullen when things didn't go his way. If only he could be as adaptable and good-natured as Sally.

Old Maria put her head in the dining-room door. Those kids—dawdling again. Especially that Bill. If he was *her* son, she'd teach him a little consideration for his elders. When it rained her bones ached and she wanted to get her work done and have some time to rest.

The main effect of that story opening is one of confusing jumpiness. The first paragraph is fine. This is going to be Bill's story. The problem is going to concern the fact that it is raining on a day when he wants to practice football. We begin to be interested. We experience a certain sympathy with Bill and we want to know what happens.

But in the second paragraph we discover that we were all wrong. This story is going to be about Sally's morning in the attic going through her grandmother's trunk. There is a letdown of interest when the story shifts from Bill's point of view, and there is an entire change of mood. But being patient, we rearrange our mental machinery and decide to go along with Sally. At the end of the paragraph about Sally, we trip over a sentence about how pretty she looks "with her big blue eyes dancing and her lips wearing a sunny smile." As Sally cannot possibly see herself like this unless she stands before a mirror, we are jerked out of viewpoint again.

In the third paragraph we find that we guessed wrong the first two times and that the story is going to be about Mrs. Hall's problem with Bill and her satisfaction with Sally. At this point the young reader tosses the story down and turns on the television because the last problem in the world to interest him is the trouble a mother is having with her children.

The adult reader may keep reading on to the fourth paragraph, where he discovers that the problem concerns an elderly servant's aching bones on a rainy day. Whereupon even he throws the story down, because he is so thoroughly confused that he doesn't know what it is all about, or whom to sympathize with—and cares even less.

Any one of the viewpoints in the above paragraphs might be suitable for a different story, depending upon what story the writer wanted to tell and what kind of audience he meant to write for. But don't cram them all into one story. Were I forced to make a choice of viewpoint character for this story, however, I'd say at once that it should be Bill, if I wanted to make it a story for children. Everything looks too bright and cheery for Sally for her viewpoint to result in a good story, while Bill is faced with Trouble in paragraph one.

When your viewpoint character is clear in your own mind, you are ready to move on to the rest of the cast. Except that you will not get into the minds of the other characters, the devices and techniques used for characterization are about the same for all your fictional people. Major characters may be built up with a fairly lavish hand; for minor characters you will perhaps select no more than a single trait which will individualize each one within the type.

There are a number of means by which characters may be portrayed to the reader. There are times when straight description must be used. If handled badly, this can bog down any story. So keep your description fresh and alive.

Remember the importance of immediacy, of something happening now. Don't *tell* the reader. Give him a picture he can see for himself. *Show* your character doing something which characterizes. Don't say, "Midge took her things off in an untidy manner." Get that picture across. Say: "Midge came in shedding sweater, ski cap, and mittens in all directions. She always rid herself of her things with an effect of buttons popping toward every point of the compass."

Dialogue is one of the most useful vehicles for the purpose of good characterization. Yet in so many first stories, all the characters sound exactly alike. Make the words your people speak bear out whatever traits of character you have chosen for them. If your heroine is a lively young person, don't talk about it—make her sound lively. If a boy character is deep in gloom—like Bill facing a rainy Saturday— then he certainly mustn't sound like your cheery heroine, or vice versa.

Most readers prefer to find lots of conversation in the stories they read. A solid page of print, unbroken by dialogue, is tiresome to the eye. What people say is just as important as what they do and every bit as interesting.

What a person says and how he or she says it is, if properly handled, an immediate key to character and will give the illusion of reality so necessary to a satisfying story.

The most important rule in the writing of dialogue is to

make it sound natural. An ear for dialogue is a valuable asset to any writer and you can develop such an ear if you listen carefully enough.

It is not always easy for an adult to make young people in a story sound the way they really do in life. You need to spend considerable time listening to children as they talk today before you can do it successfully. Remembering is not good enough because speech idioms change with the passing of years. Check your own slang habits and don't permit in your story phrases which were commonly used when you were a child. Just because they sound natural to you, it does not mean that they will be understood by today's youngsters, let alone used by them.

In the matter of slang, a moderate amount may be used to give naturalness to conversation, but it is wiser to avoid the short-lived catch phrase of the moment. It may be dated by the time your story sees print, and in a book is likely to seem archaic in a year or two. In one story I had a character refer to "the sixty-four dollar question." At the time of writing there were few youngsters in America who would not understand that phrase. But how long it would be meaningful was a matter of conjecture. I decided to delete it. A good thing. That book is still in print, but young people today have never heard of that famous question.

I used to think young people would go on saying "swell" forever. The word seemed to have become a part of the language in America. Now I'm not so sure. There are other words, and you'd better be aware of them. It isn't all that hard to write without using current slang, yet still keep your young characters sounding natural. Ghetto language, street language, is something else; if you are to convey current reality it may be necessary to use some of the real words. Just don't start sounding like a foreign language that not all your readers will understand.

Having what you write get out of date can be a problem. I never dreamed that my books would still be in print thirty and more years after I wrote them. The black characters in *Willow Hill* are still called Negroes, but the book has dated little in other ways. The basic problems, the human elements, remain the same. You can't outguess the future, and you must write for *now*. But if the doubtful word can be avoided, standard English is a better choice.

By all means, read your dialogue aloud. It is good practice, in fact, to read your entire story out loud. Many phrases which look fine in type sound awkward when spoken. Use shortened forms; loosen up your characters' speech; avoid stiffness and formality. Use the words each character would be likely to say. And show by the things the character says what manner of person he or she is.

It is a good exercise to check the dialogue in the stories of skilled writers and study how well character may be revealed through speech.

There are a few minor matters to watch. Just as solid pages of unbroken print are tiresome to the eye, long passages of dialogue spoken by one character can be equally so. In the course of ordinary conversation, few children make long speeches without interruption. If it is necessary for a character to tell a long story, have other characters break in from time to time, or interrupt the talk with some bit of action. Never let your character get up on a soap box.

Don't be afraid of "cueing" your dialogue. "He said" is a perfectly good phrase, but some writers become so afraid of repeating it that they go to fantastic lengths to substitute other words. It is annoying to a reader to follow a page where the author has used in rotation, "he admitted," "she confided," "he enjoined," "she hazarded," "he boasted," "she mimicked," and so on. The reader begins to long for just one simple "said." It is true that too many "saids" in a row can also intrude, but they are to be preferred to the above method.

Perhaps the best method is to use "saids" and occasional "said" substitutes, arriving at variety by rearranging your sentence structure.

Don't always use the common form:

"I'm awfully sorry about being late again, Mrs. Farmer," Mary Blake said, coming down from her high horse in a split second.

Try it again this way:

Mary Blake came down from her high horse in a split second. "I'm awfully sorry about being late again, Mrs. Farmer."

Above all, don't use substitutes for "said" like "beamed," in the following sentence:

"I think the drawing is beautiful," Polly beamed.

I'd like to see anyone *beam* a sentence.

The important thing is not to leave your reader in the dark as to which character is speaking. Even when there are only two people on the scene it can become very confusing after a few speeches if the author does no cueing.

It is a valuable help to start collecting juvenile characters in that notebook you carry around in your pocket or purse. Don't put down a feature-by-feature description of the little girl sitting across from you on the bus. It doesn't matter that she has blue eyes and blond hair. Look for the *significant*. Do her eyes examine her fellow passengers with lively interest? Or does her attention dart here and there in a frightened way? Is her blond hair limp and bedraggled, or has someone brushed it into shining smoothness? These are the things which give you the significant, characterizing detail. She is wearing brown sandals, perhaps. Nothing significant about that. But let the sandals be polished to brilliance despite worn tips, have the dress clean but obviously mended, and we have an idea of the child's background. So on through every detail of appearance and manner. What is her voice like? How does she stand? How does she walk? What is her manner as she speaks to the friends with her? What can you read about her from all these signs?

It will take a little practice at first, but if you stay with it you'll develop a knack for distinguishing the significant at a glance, and you'll have a wealth of material to draw from when you need it.

We learn to characterize, not only by watching others, but by observing ourselves. No day of our lives passes without our being stirred to some emotion. We are pleased, annoyed, embarrassed, moved to tears or laughter. Get the habit of looking at yourself objectively and finding out what makes you click. Was your impatience justified? Why were you so ridiculously pleased over that casual word of praise? Or unreasonably hurt by so small a slight? Understand these things in yourself, and you will be better able to understand your characters. Emotional reactions are not very different, whether you are writing about children or adults. Perhaps emotions are simpler and more spontaneous, less self-conscious in childhood. Joys are keener, disappointments sharper. But out of your own joys and disappointments you can learn to understand the emotions of your characters.

When you want to portray an unpleasant character, try giving him some of your own faults. Our faults as adults had their beginnings when we were children. We can see the unpleasant aspect of those faults and at the same time understand why they came into being and what difficulties they may cause. As a result, your young character is more likely to be real and believable. Oddly enough, in answering a questionnaire I used in my writing classes, there are always several students who say they are not aware that they have any bad habits. My recommendation to those lucky individuals was to give up writing. Your faults are part of your stock-in-trade as a writer; this is one area, in fact, where they can stand you in good stead. Better recognize them and use them.

Conversely, here is your opportunity to extol all those virtues you felt went unappreciated by dull grownups when you were a child. There is a universality about good behavior and bad which belongs to both the juvenile and the adult world. We feel very much the same emotions a child feels, but as adults we have learned to control and repress some of them, so that we are less primitive in our expression of them. The fundamental psychological needs we had as children grew up with us and became more controlled.

Let us say that by now you have your characters drawn clearly in your own mind. You are nearly ready to set them down on paper in a story. Don't begin writing until you have decided what role each character is to play in your reader's emotions. This advice may seem so obvious that you are likely to dismiss it as something you already know. Are you sure?

You say you want your reader to be sympathetically inclined toward Mary Jones; that the emotions you wish to arouse in your readers are first, liking, then tolerant amusement, becoming finally admiration at the close of the story. However, on page six, your fictional girl steps completely out of character and reveals a flash of bad temper for which you had not prepared your readers, thus losing their liking for her that you had meant to build up.

"But," you may say, "by having her show her bad temper,

I am only making her human. I thought I was supposed to give her contradictory traits."

Right. You were. But see to it that those contradictory traits still contribute to the general impression you want to make upon the reader. Her faults had better be minor ones; she can be mistaken in her views, or in some action she takes, but she mustn't be petty and bad-tempered—not if you want to keep her sympathetic throughout the story, and build up to the admiration you want for this particular girl at the end.

Another thing: Don't set your characters down in a void. Richness of background is one of the most useful means of bringing a story to life. By "richness" I don't mean the sumptuous. I mean richness of sensory detail. Background may help to characterize your people, either by suiting them, or by contrasting incongruously. There is something challenging to reader interest about a well-dressed girl in a shabby setting, or a shabby girl against a luxurious background, and the very contrast will serve to characterize when we learn the why behind it, or how a character behaves in an incongruous setting.

Too often beginners' stories take place in a vacuum, and they forget entirely about appealing to the readers' senses. This is important in writing for adults, but in children's stories it is imperative. Children understand much of what goes on around them through their senses, and skillful writers use sensory detail to a marked degree in writing for young people. Always remember to use sensory references as much as possible in your writing, not in long unrelieved paragraphs of description, but by weaving them unobtrusively through the action and dialogue in your story.

Characterization is not something you do only when one of your fictional people first walks onstage. In story after story, flat, descriptive statements tend to be used. A character is tall, dark, and handsome; he has laughing eyes and gleaming teeth (or is it the other way around?), but thereafter all "characterizing" touches are abandoned for the remainder of the story. He becomes an invisible nonentity who makes speeches that sound just like all the speeches made by other nonentities, whom we distinguish from one another, male or female, young or old, only by name.

Characterization is something you do *consistently* with every character every time he appears on a scene.

That word *"consistently"* is the important word. Perhaps more than any other one fault inconsistency of characterization will bring rejection slips. In the early part of a story Johnny is a mule-stubborn little boy who wants what he wants—or else. At the climax, he yields amiably to the wishes of another character, at no little cost to himself. And the editor writes "characterization not consistent" on a rejection slip and sends it back. It isn't that Johnny could not change in the course of a story, provided that the character change and the reason behind it are carefully developed along the way. But when a character does a broad jump from here to yon for no other reason than to suit the author's whim, then the characterization is certainly inconsistent.

It is at this point that the measuring stick I mentioned earlier comes in. The test is a simple one, but it is tremendously important. Take each paragraph of your story in turn and analyze it. What characters are on the scene at that point? Does that paragraph individualize each of those characters in the scene? Does every paragraph contribute in some way to the readers' understanding of each character as a person? Is this done consistently?

If your hero is a tough little egg on page one, only to sound like a sissy on page two, you aren't visualizing him very clearly yourself and you are certainly confusing your reader. If you find that your picture is blurred and all your characters have run together in an indistinguishable mass, then sit down and introduce consistent characterization throughout the story.

No character must be goody-goody; no character must be thoroughly bad. No living child belongs to either extreme. Look for faults in your good characters, and make sure that your bad ones have virtues, and you'll be much more likely to write about children as they are.

Again I'd like to warn you to keep adult characters out of the story as much as possible. Your young readers are interested in young characters, and they don't give a whoop about Aunt Josie's romance, or about the disaster that is about to befall Uncle Ned. *Not unless those things very strongly affect their own interests.* Above all, whether you are writing a short story or a book, get your major characters into the scene as early as you possibly can. Don't drag them in by their heels at the last minute because you need them in the climax scene. Recently, a book manuscript came to me for criticism in which the hero of this teen-age novel for girls came into the story when the book was three-quarters over. When I protested, the author told me that the hero really wasn't "very important." But your teen-age readers want a hero who *is* important, and they want to know about him right away. It may not be that the hero's importance is recognized immediately, but he should certainly be in evidence from the first.

One final warning, and in this no one can help you. You can do almost automatically all the things I have set down in this chapter. They will help you make your fictional children real. But there is one bit of magic which only you can breathe into this collection of features and traits you create, build up, name, and call a character.

Somehow, before your straw man comes to life, you must

by empathy get yourself into his skin. Empathy, according to Rebecca West's definition, is "our power of projecting ourselves into the destiny of others by fantasy."

I have gone through the disheartening experience of drawing a character who should have carried a conviction of life, but who somehow behaved in a forced and wooden manner when he stepped out on my story stage. I had not succeeded in projecting myself into his destiny. This I cannot tell you how to do. I only know that it must be done and that all these other elements of technique will help greatly to put you in a position where you can work the final magic yourself. Then the young people who pick up your story will read with delight, knowing they are meeting other youngsters as real as themselves; new friends they will want to keep, whose experiences they will profit by long after they have put your story down.

9 | PLOT

All the time that you are working with your characters, plot material will be coming to life, almost without effort. The desire and characteristics of one character clash with those of another, and plot ideas begin to develop. On the other hand, when you begin to work directly with plot, you will find that your situations, your story problem, your theme, all require certain types of characters to handle them. It is quite likely that the exigencies of your plot will cause you to rework some of your characters.

It is equally likely that as your characters come to life and new plot incidents develop, you may want to change the framework of your plan. One affects the other, both are interwoven, and, as I have said, of *equal* importance.

By all means, while you are planning your story—even while you are writing it—keep your material flexible. Don't feel that you are making a plaster cast with rigid outlines from which you must never depart. Within the boundaries of certain laws which you will be wiser to allow to govern your story-telling, feel always that you can change anything anywhere along the line. Don't reject the new idea with which your subconscious suddenly provides you. Make it welcome and see if it might improve your story, even if it is something which did not come into your first planning.

Quite often a plotting impasse grows out of planning too

rigidly and tying ourselves into such knots that we miss seeing the loose end lying right at hand, which we have only to tug to untie and untangle everything. I recall the difficulties one writer got himself into simply because at a certain point in his story he required a window through which a character could make an escape. When the need for such a window was pointed out to him, he protested that no such window existed in the building he had in mind. His imaginary conception of the scene was so clear to him that he forgot it was up to him as the creator to put a window wherever he wanted one. It is fine to imagine things as vividly as that, but not to the extent that doing so hampers you when there are changes that need to be made.

Plot, as a rule, is the bugaboo of every beginner. The word seems to imply the need of some very special knack, some highly developed skill. All the other elements of writing appear easy to learn, but an ogre of grimmest mien guards the mysterious gateway to plotting. And right before that entrance a good many writers put down their pens and flee.

Which is very silly indeed, because the ogre is quite imaginary. A plot is only a plan—a method of organizing your material so that it will accomplish what you want a story to do: that is, to interest and move the reader. This takes a little discipline, a bit of practice, but once you understand the purpose and use of plot in a story, it should never defeat you again. To reach an audience, any art needs an understandable form. A plot, a plan, will give you that form.

Your subconscious conjures up this specter to frighten you away. "You can't possibly plot," this fearful ogre whispers. "Besides, it takes a crass commercial sense to work out mechanical stuff like that. You are an Artist. You can create character; you can write the most gorgeous descriptions.

But plotting—no. Keep away from anything so lowbrow as that. And anyway, you couldn't plot, even if you tried."

But there is no need to—and you must not—let your subconscious or anything else discourage you about plotting. Anyone with a moderate amount of intelligence and imagination can learn to plot a story. The only terrifying thing about it is that this is the point at which you really have to go to work and *think*. You have to concentrate intently. If your early training has prepared you for this, you have an ace in your favor. If you find that when you start trying to think about your plot your mind gets off on the grocery list, or that tooth that ought to be filled, or where you mean to spend your next vacation, or any number of other irrelevant matters, you are going to have to do a little persistent training right now. So let's get on with it.

Have a clock at hand. Make yourself comfortable. My choice is to stretch out on a couch at full length if I want to plot during the day. Sometimes I do it just before I go to sleep at night, but my purpose then is a little different and the thinking at night must be approached with some caution or you will find yourself so wide awake that you won't get to sleep for hours.

The clock is necessary in the beginning for training purposes. Later on, you can dispense with it. At first you will need to time yourself in order to hold sternly to the work in hand. The first day you should think for at least five minutes straight about your story. It will be harder than you imagine. Every time the grocery list or anything else tries to crowd in, you are going to push it right out of your consciousness and pull your attention back to that story. Every time your mind wanders, start your five minutes over again, until you get in an uninterrupted stretch. Increase the time from day to day, depending upon the progress you make.

It is a help, I think, to close your eyes, even to put your palms over your eyes until you see nothing but black. *Think* black for a few seconds. Whisper the word "black" over and over until there is nothing in your mind but soothing darkness. Then turn on the film and start watching your story people act out a scene. When you have practiced this intensive concentration over a period of several weeks, months, years, you will find that you can turn that story reel on whenever you want to and hold your attention to it for as long a time as you care to spend. After a while, you won't need to go through the rigmarole of closing your eyes or lying down; you'll find you can concentrate any time at all. You can do it while you're scrubbing in the tub, or riding on a bus or while you're crossing the street in the midst of heavy traffic. You are likely to pass your best friends by on the street because you're far away in your story and don't even see them; and you are likely to increase your growing reputation for being odd, but that's all right: This is plotting.

It is not something which can be completed in an hour or two; it is not something which can be pushed or hurried. It is something which grows and develops gradually as you feed more and more ideas to your subconscious. They will be jelling while you aren't thinking about them at all; they'll be growing while you sleep.

Every day you sort over the new material with which your subconscious has provided you in return for the odds and ends you have fed it, and see what you can do by way of fitting it into a prescribed story pattern. When your mind balks and a scene refuses to develop, it may mean that you have been trying to force your material into an unnatural pattern which your subconscious is rejecting. Try to get a new slant on that particular scene or problem, a new approach. Examine all its elements, explore new paths it may take. The trouble may be only that at this point you have not doled out enough new and stimulating story germs, so that your mind hasn't enough to work on to develop the scene. If that is the case, it is a good idea to read a book about the subject you're working on, or get out into the field and see what data you can collect to stimulate your imagination.

When a problem really stumps me, I try thinking about it just before I go to sleep. I do *not* try to figure it out completely at that time, because I know only too well that doing so would only wake me up and probably would not solve the difficulty at all. I spend a few minutes shifting the problem to my subconscious, determined that by the next day I am going to find my difficulty solved. I hold myself to that line of thought as nearly as possible without deviating, until I fall asleep.

I don't want to be esoteric or wave magic wands under your nose, but if there is any magic to this matter of being a writer, it rests in the use you make of your subconscious. The above-mentioned method is, of course, psychologically sound, and has been proved so many times by people in almost every line of work that it needs no apology or defense.

Don't try to push your mind into doing this work for you. It isn't necessary to be grimly determined about it. Nor can you approach it with doubt and despair. Quiet confidence is the attitude that you must achieve. You must believe without any doubt that this approach will work, and you must fall asleep repeating your conviction over and over in your mind.

When morning comes, don't expect to be awakened by trumpets which announce that the answer has been provided and is there waiting for you. Don't expect any blinding revelations. In fact, it is possible that the next time you think of the problem, it will look just as knotty as ever. When you go back to your desk and recall some vague idea that you'd touched on uncertainly yesterday, you find that today it sounds more sensible. You get to work and without any fanfare, perhaps without conscious realization, the problem works itself out. You may even say, "But I had that in mind all along. It wasn't any subconscious nonsense that figured that out." Nevertheless, yesterday you were stuck, and today you are moving ahead.

It doesn't always happen as quickly as that. Sometimes the process may take much longer than twenty-four hours; sometimes you may have to put that particular problem aside and turn your immediate attention to some other angle of your story or another chapter of your novel—or even to another book. But, sooner or later, unless you are forcing something totally inappropriate, the answer will appear, and you'll be over another hump.

I find it a help, even when my next scene is so thoroughly planned that no problem exists, to try to fall asleep knowing that I will be able to handle that scene satisfactorily when I return to my typewriter the next morning.

At first, you will have to make a special effort to do this, but after a while—like the other elements of fiction writing —it will become so much a part of your working method that you will do it automatically without thinking much about it, except for those occasions when your material turns unusually stubborn.

I worked out this method for myself more than thirty years ago and still use the same approach to get me through all plotting difficulties. Sometimes the answers come in a spectacular fashion, as they did for me when I was trying to get myself out of a blank place while I was writing my East Hampton adult novel, *The Golden Unicorn*.

I was as thoroughly stumped in writing that book as I've

ever been. Two-thirds of the way through, I had to get five characters from East Hampton to Montauk Point for several reasons I needn't go into now. Yet I could think of nothing interesting to do with them once I got them there. This problem showed up early in my planning stages. I simply wrote it down as a question to be solved later. Eventually the time came when it had to be solved, yet no prodding of the subconscious came up with an answer. The scene, of course, would have to be necessary to the plot. Something must happen which would help the story and make the scene vitally important.

As I've said before, there is always a way. You just keep knocking on the door. So, having reached the place where I couldn't continue writing, I did what often helps. I went back and reread the manuscript from the beginning.

There are three steps in making use of the subconscious. (This method doesn't always work immediately, and you may need to give it more than one try.)

1. Put an idea or problem into the mind. Ask a question.
2. Forget about it and turn to something else.
3. Bring it out later and examine it for an answer.

In this case, rereading what I'd written became the means of putting a lot of material back into my mind. I didn't worry about the problem, or look consciously for a solution, but just let it alone and worked at revision. By the time I came to the sticking point in my reading, I still had no answer.

After lunch on the day I finished the reading, I lay down for a nap. Before I fell asleep, I considered a little tentatively the problem that still faced me—*and the whole thing was there!* In a flash in all its detail I found a valuable turn to the plot, a new character I hadn't thought of before, answers to various ticklish, related plot problems, and a whole dramatic scene that would move the story forward. It took only moments for me to see all this. I got up and put it all down in notes before it could get away from me. Very little revision was needed to work the new material in, because it was all there—embedded in what had gone before, though I hadn't been able to see it with my conscious mind. Even the new character was hidden in what I had previously set on paper. Miraculously, something had put it all together and presented me with exactly what I needed.

Over the years, this system has worked for me, and I'd advise you to cultivate it for yourself. The answers don't always come as spectacularly as in this instance. It's not necessary for bells to ring and horns to blow. Your "answer" can come very quietly. Nor do I use this method always just before I fall asleep. Whenever I want an answer to some question about a story, however small, I lie down, close my eyes—and *watch*. When I get up—perhaps only ten minutes later—something will have come clear.

So much for the "hard" part of plotting. The rest is easier because it is technical and mechanical. There are certain things you must accomplish in every story you write. Once you understand these points, you will have no particular difficulty fitting your material into the best possible form.

There are many ways in which you may put your story or novel together. At this point, dogma of any kind is dangerous. One writer's method, however sound and sensible, may not work for another. In the beginning, if you can train yourself to one of the better, time-saving methods, you may save yourself a great deal of grief later on. When you become thoroughly conditioned to one writing method and then try to force yourself into a different pattern of work, you may be hindered and inhibited so that your imagination will not work at all.

Some people think easily of climax scenes first and then

work backward to get an opening and the rest of the preceding scenes. Others take no interest whatsoever in climaxes until they have thought through all the beginning steps.

But, however you start putting things together, try to make an outline first. There are writers who work by the sit-down-and-dash-it-off method, but usually they have the kind of fast-moving minds in which some sort of outline is dashing on ahead of the scene they are writing and is ready when they come to it. Really good workers who write by this method are rare, and the second-rate stories turned out by the nonplanners show the lack of planning. Often a great deal of revision is needed.

I won't quarrel with your manner of outlining, so long as you do outline. Some writers work best with an outline which is completely mental; others like to do it completely on paper. Still others get results by talking their ideas over with someone else. All three methods have advantages and disadvantages, and you may work out a combination of the three.

The "mental" outline has an advantage in that it does not take the edge off the writing itself. If you can think your story through *completely* from beginning to end, you are almost sure to approach the writing with a feeling of freshness and adventure. Unfortunately, this type of outline is apt to get a little blurred in some important details because you rush over some troublesome point that is not down on paper. Then you start writing, reach that point, and get stuck right there. All your interest in the story dies out, you become bored with it, and unless you exert a great deal of discipline, you will find yourself putting it aside as a failure and going on to some fresher and more appealing idea. It is all too easy to become a "beginner" and not a "finisher." If you are troubled by this drop in interest a few pages after the start of your story, the difficulty probably lies in a lack of careful planning. The mental outline, like any other, is good only if it is complete. For a book it is scarcely to be considered because it would be impossible for most minds to hold such a bulk of material in view by that method.

The written outline is undoubtedly the best. Some writers claim that once they have worked over an outline they feel they have written the story and all their zest for the actual writing is gone. There is something in this, and I remember very well using the same excuse myself. Mainly, however, I believe that it is a matter of poor conditioning. I can do a great deal of outlining without having it interfere in the least with the writing of the story. You will be better off if you condition yourself to working with an outline.

Although this method worked for me for a long time, it has gradually changed, until my outlines now are pared down to a bare minimum. More on this later.

It can be very helpful to talk over various aspects of a story with people whose judgment you can trust and whose views are sympathetic, though not necessarily always in agreement with yours. I believe, however, that you can do this safely only when you have the confidence of success behind you. Nothing anyone can say will then throw you so completely off that you cannot write the story.

With the beginner that may easily happen. I have seen too many books go into the discard pile simply because the writers talked about them too much while they were writing them. One person gives you one opinion, another contradicts the first, and as many views on a subject can be found as there are people to consult. The result for writers may be such confusion that they will not be able to write their books at all. This can be just as true in the short story, and it is often better to get your idea down on paper, get it done first—and then do your talking. This may seem wasteful of your time, but at least you will then have a finished piece of work to look at, discuss, analyze, and, if necessary, tear apart and reassemble without being thrown off so that you cannot complete the story.

However you manage it—outline to some extent. If you don't, you are very likely to find yourself painting a lovely shade of blue on a wall that does not exist, or building a fireplace with no chimney above it, or getting your house completed, only to find that you've forgotten the stairs. Then it will take a real tearing down to rebuild.

After all, you can't put up so much as your front door unless you know whether you mean to build a firehouse, a grocery store, or a Hollywood mansion. Your outline gives you the blueprint for your house and settles a great many matters before you get to the point of laying the cornerstone.

In building a plot, what you feed your imagination first does not matter very much. It may be a character, a theme, a situation, a setting, a job, a hobby—anything at all. But once you get the story or novel stirring, with bits coming to life here and there, you must decide definitely and clearly on your story problem. What does your main character want? How much depends on his success? What events and people oppose him? (It must never be easy for him, or you'll have no suspense.) What does he do to overcome these obstacles? How does he *by his own action* solve his problem? When you have answered those questions, you have a "plot." It's as hard as that. If you leave any of these questions unanswered or omit them, your story framework will not be strong enough, and it will lack plot.

Suppose we look at these questions individually with special regard to writing for young people.

What does your main character want? Be sure it is something very much desired. Make the problem one to which the readers for whom the story or novel is intended would be sympathetic. Make the goal important, not one that is too easy or trivial. A young girl who wants to learn to be liked can be made a very sympathetic character, but a girl who wants to be the belle of the ball so that she can draw the attention of the boys away from the other girls has a motive too petty to be made the heroine. Don't, however, give your main character a goal or desire so noble that real young people could not relate to it (however admirable it may seem to adults), or you will lose your audience on page one.

Be sure the character's goal is specific, not something general like, "I want to find happiness." That is too vague and abstract. Perhaps it's what all stories and novels are about, but you need to pin down some one phase of the abstract goal that you can state simply.

How much depends on your main character's getting what he wants? It must *matter*. Your readers must care what happens; their sympathies as readers must be strongly in favor of having your hero achieve his aim, because of the unhappiness which would result from his failure to do so.

What events and people oppose him? His ultimate success must never be easy. Getting your main character in continual hot water is one of the secrets of suspense. So much must be stacked against this person that the possibility of success is in doubt at several points in your story or novel. If the girl who wants to be liked decides to be more pleasant and interested in other people and starts right off to do so, and other people begin to like her, you have no obstacles to having her solve her problem—no conflict, no story.

When you have decided on the obstacles, what does your

main character do to overcome them by his or her own efforts? How does your hero or heroine reveal whatever admirable characteristics you have given him or her in the course of their struggle for success? Of course, before one obstacle is overcome, you must introduce another, so that your reader is carried along from scene to scene, always eager to know what will happen next. The moment you leave readers satisfied, with no further questions in their minds, your story or novel is over, whether you want it to be or not.

How does your hero finally solve his problem *by his own actions?* This is important. Too often problems in fiction are solved by chance. Someone other than the hero comes along fortuitously and saves the day, getting your hero neatly out of his scrape. But if your hero is going to be a hero, he has to get out of his own scrapes. Luck can play a greater part in real life than it can in fiction.

If something just happens, if your hero doesn't achieve his goal through his own efforts and actions, your story or novel will not have a satisfying climax. And if there is one rule that writers for children must learn and use, it is this: the ending must satisfy. It is much easier to leave your reader with the feeling that All Is Futility than it is to work out a satisfactory solution that helps give him the confidence to go ahead and solve his own problems.

Young readers like to have problems logically solved. They want something from fiction they can take away and use in their own lives whenever possible. We should not forget that a story or novel can be for fun, and that it can offer hope. In some of the dark realism which pictures the hopeless and tragic, we may do more harm than good, unless we remember to offer the reader hope.

There is, however, room for all kinds of writing and all kinds of readers in the juvenile field. Not only happy endings are allowed in fiction. Readers can find satisfaction in tears. Not everything needs to turn out exactly right at the end of a story. But there must still be hope, or life is worthless.

Your solution, whatever it is, must result from your main character's action. No other person in your story or novel can solve the problem for the hero or heroine. Because of the kind of person you have created in your leading character, he or she performs some action which solves the problem. You cannot have the action of another character make your hero "come to realize" that he has been mistaken and then determine to do better from then on.

In a sense, perhaps, all stories which show character change have come-to-realize plots. The point which must be kept in mind is that the character comes to this state of realization out of his own action—not because someone else tells him he must do better, so that he merely changes his mind.

There are three definite steps to be considered in using the come-to-realize ending successfully:

1. The main character has been following a mistaken course, is trying to solve a problem in the wrong way. No good advice from others is listened to, no opposition accepted. Then, toward the end of the story, *something happens* to cause this character to recognize the mistake he or she has been making. This "something" must come in the form of dramatic action. The hero or heroine is in fact *shocked* into coming-to-realize. If someone just tells the hero the way out and he agrees, your ending will be weak and unsatisfactory.

2. Having been shocked into recognition of the error of his ways, the character now stops to think and "realize" —but not for too long. If, however, at this point he de-

cides to change his course of action and the story just ends there, you will again have a weak story, and your readers will feel unsatisfied. In fact, they won't really believe that your character is going to change.

3. Thus you need the third and final step. Your main character now *takes action* himself and *does something* to prove that he has changed. This action can be small or large. It may or may not be the climax of the story, but it must be in your story if you want to leave a satisfied reader.

Avoid the come-to-realize ending unless you can handle it in the proper way. Study published stories and books for the handling of this element. It is useful and you needn't fear it if you follow the three steps.

There must, of course, be action in fiction for young people. This does not mean that something wildly exciting must happen on every page, but more a sense of having something going on and an underlying promise that the exciting is about to happen. This can often be achieved in a scene where there is no *physical* action going on at all.

Think of your story as a series of scenes being presented on a stage. In your planning, break it up into four or five parts, each, if possible, laid against a different background. A change of scene may mean no more than a shift to another room, but it always adds interest to the story. If your transitions are quickly and smoothly accomplished, these changes of background will give your story a flowing movement that carries it on toward the climax. It may be necessary to return at times to a scene previously presented, but usually there is a difference as to time of day or people "on stage," which will keep it from being repetitive. A story that begins in one room and continues in the same setting to the end of the story can be very monotonous.

The time element must be considered in your planning. In a short story don't begin when your heroine was three years old and have her grow up in the first few pages so that your story covers a long period of years. Very few stories will not be improved by having them start as close to the time of the climax as possible. Two or three days may well be sufficient time for your story to happen, or even two or three hours, though of course your material will guide you to a great extent in this. Usually, however, all that vital information that makes you want to start the action several months or years before the climax can be woven into the first paragraphs, if you give enough thought and effort to the matter.

In your planning, watch always for the trite and the obvious and reject them for something more unusual. The idea that comes most easily is to be regarded with suspicion. Your subconscious is merely trying to put something over on you. You have read the same idea many times and stored it away in your subconscious, and you won't have to work very hard to bring it to the conscious level. When you say, "Come on, produce," all you have to do is call on your subconscious to come up with this overworked idea. But you must learn to say sternly, "This is so shopworn, nobody will want it—including me." So you get busy and this time dig down a little farther into the subconscious storeroom and come up with something new and fresh.

You are the boss.

The exception to this is the trite situation that you reverse or change around so that the effect is fresh and unexpected. For example, Cinderella is a mess, a greedy climber, and one of the older sisters really deserves the prince. Almost any cliché situation can be turned inside out, so experiment, and surprise both yourself and the reader. In *Mystery of the Black Diamonds,* I used the age-old treasure hunt. But my characters find the treasure in the middle of the book, instead of at the end, and when they have it they don't know what it is. So the mystery continues.

Before concluding this chapter on plot, I want to return to that plot notebook I mentioned earlier as one notebook I kept up faithfully all through my short story writing days. Almost anything that will provide an idea may go into that book. You may have a section for themes, for characters, for unusual hobbies—anything at all that may stimulate your imagination. But I kept more than this kind of note in my book; I kept a list of plot situations that ran into the hundreds, and I could always draw from them when the well began to run dry.

If you are going to write fiction for children, you must of course keep reading juvenile stories and novels being written by other writers. This will help you keep in the mood and aware of the current market. From every story or novel I read, I separated the germinal situation, free of all its story trappings, and set it down in my notebook. Scanning a few pages, I find such items as the following:

> A girl sets out to teach someone a lesson and learns the same lesson herself.
> A girl discovers that you can't dislike people, once you get to know them. (This simple truth is the theme of *Willow Hill,* which won a prize.)
> A girl is so intent upon a goal she wants to reach that she misses the fact that it is more important to enjoy the road which leads to that goal.
> A group of young people find themselves in desperate circumstances, only to have the one person in the group whom they have previously scorned provide the way out.

You can make your own list. Boil every story you read down to the very germ that tells what it is about. You are not going to be interested in how that particular writer worked the story out; in fact, you must be very sure that you follow no one else's beaten path. Collect so many of these plot situations that you forget what the original stories were about. Then, when you are in need of a story idea, feed a few of them to your imagination, and see what clicks. A hundred writers could take the above situations and each write a story without having any of the hundred stories resemble one another. The possibilities are limitless. When you use this method, you can start off happily with the first step taken toward your plot. You can write down in one sentence what your story is going to be about—which should always be your first step in story writing.

Another section of your notebook may be given over to "opening situations." These may resemble the germinal plots to some extent, but there is a difference, since these will present you with your opening scene ready made. Here are two from my collection:

> A young librarian is feeling hemmed in by books, longing for wider horizons and more contact with life.
> A girl comes home to a situation where she knows she isn't wanted.

Obviously, it is more useful and stimulating for you to collect your own items.

Beginning with a situation has still another advantage in that you are immediately presented with two or more characters. All you need to do is start getting acquainted with them and find out why that situation faces them and what they mean to do about it.

However you manage it, keep the idea reservoir constantly replenished, and don't let the ogre of plot frighten you. If you keep your subconscious well fed with story ideas, if you plan your story carefully so that the questions in this chapter are answered, you need have little worry about learning to plot.

10 PUTTING IT TOGETHER

A plotted story will break naturally into the following sections:

> Opening
> Body
> Climax
> Denouement

Thinking of your story as a series of scenes, you will assign one scene to the opening, possibly a single scene to climax and denouement together, though this is not necessarily a rule, and the remainder of your scenes to the body of the story.

Each of these sections is important, and the misuse of any one of them can ruin the effect of your story. The opening, however, is your show window, and you must put your best effort into that. You have just one chance to catch the interest of your young reader. That chance lies on your first page. It may even lie in your first paragraph. No matter what exciting things you know are going to happen on page six, your reader (and incidentally the editor) will not stay with you that long unless on page one you sell him the idea of reading more.

There are various methods of beginning a story and your material will to some extent govern this. But when it comes to technique, the wise author does more governing than being governed. Whatever your choice of methods of opening your story or novel, remember that your problem should be made clear to your reader as soon as possible—so clear, that in your planning process, you will have written it down in a sentence or two and will never thereafter forget what *this* story is supposed to be about. It isn't always possible to get the problem stated completely on the first page, but you can weave in direct leads which point to it. When you do so, readers know immediately that there *is* a problem, and that the main character is trying to do something about it.

There are four ways in which a story or novel may open: narrative, dialogue, with one character thinking, or one or more characters doing something interesting. Sometimes we use a combination of several of these methods.

I used to be strongly opposed to using narrative or exposition openings, i.e., the author *telling* the reader. However, in checking back over the opening paragraphs of my novels for young people, reading first paragraphs only, I find that narrative can serve a writer very well, particularly in the opening of a novel.

Here is the beginning paragraph in my *Secret of the Haunted Mesa:*

> The red heart of the campfire centered the night scene and made it pulse with a crimson glow. Juniper wood gave off a pungent scent that was pleasant on the air. Around the fire, logs and beams had been placed, offering seats for those who gathered near. The girl with flowing blond hair sat where firelight fell upon her lovely, uptilted face as she sang, her guitar resting on her knees. Circling the fire, the others sat quietly, watching the girl, listening to her music.

This, of course, being the opening to a novel, can take a more leisurely pace than you can afford in a short story.

In this case, I've used narrative description, from the objective viewpoint, looking on. A setting and mood are established, rather romantic and appealing to young people, and the scene is not static. Something is going on; there are people there, and one has a sense of anticipation about whatever is going to happen. In the second paragraph, I stop being objective and get inside the heroine, so that all the rest of the book is seen through her eyes, in the third person. A problem immediately makes itself known in the second paragraph, and the story begins.

The narrative type of opening will not be as active and dramatic as some, but it can have a very real appeal. It also helps you to give the reader a glimpse of place, time of day, perhaps season, and to describe your main character before you get inside her. (In the above example, the blond girl isn't the main character, but you can often focus on your hero or heroine in this way.)

Here is another narrative opening of a different type, from *Secret of the Missing Footprint*. In this case, the main character is "telling the reader":

> The day I met Timothy Rainbow my whole life changed. I don't suppose I'll ever be the same again. At first, even though he fascinated me, I thought he was a dangerous boy— but that was before he became a much more dangerous friend. In the end. . . . But I can't tell you sensibly about the end until you understand the beginning.

The interest of this opening speaks for itself, and it is wholly concerned with character. We have no idea of the setting or time.

One warning: Dialogue openings are seldom interesting. How can you be interested in what people are saying when they are complete strangers, and you don't know who they are or what they are doing? I have always paid attention to this advice; not one of my young people's books begins straight off with dialogue. This, of course, is taking into account first paragraphs only. Once my characters are introduced, the setting and time given, I try to get in some dialogue on the first page, when it is possible.

Here is an opening paragraph from my juvenile novel, *Secret of the Spotted Shell,* that combines narrative with action—a character shown doing something interesting.

> No one had come to meet her plane that afternoon at the airport in St. Thomas. Wendy Williams stood in the square box of an airport building, clearly in view, looking very neat and proper in her pleated navy blue skirt and white blouse, with a navy beret pinned to her short, dark hair. But Wendy's blue eyes, fringed with thick lashes, looked more than a little worried.

In that first sentence there is setting, time and a problem. Then we go on to the girl.

In the opening paragraph from *Secret of the Emerald Star,* which follows, we have a main character thinking:

> It was perfectly clear to Robin Ward that the family conference was not going well. The discussion concerned what she wanted to do more than anything else in the world, but Mother and Dad, and even her brother, Tommy, who was only nine, were arguing and quietly determined, all in the same breath.

In that excerpt, it is obvious that a problem is in the making, and talk, action, setting, etc., with plenty of conflict, will follow.

The following is another bit of an action opening from *Mystery of the Green Cat:*

> Without leaving his place by the wide living room window, Andy could hear angry sounds coming from across the hall.

A slamming of drawers and a general banging was going on in the bedroom Andy shared with his twin brother, Adrian.

The quicker you can get in a hint of conflict, the better. In this opening from *Mystery of the Strange Traveler*, something is happening right away. A little *motion* is always a good idea:

> Something with sharp corners pressed into Laurie's cheek and she awoke as the train jolted to a stop. It was dark in her upper berth, but she knew where she was at once. All the Kanes woke up like that, quickly and clear-headedly—all except her sister Celia, who was never sure of her own name till she'd been up for a half hour or so. Undoubtedly, Celia was still asleep in the berth below.

Those good old "W's" they told you about in English class still hold: Who? What? Where? When? Why? Those are the things you must get to quickly in the first paragraphs of your story. The "Why" is sometimes the most difficult to explain clearly and gracefully. Watch in your reading to see how it is done, and always watch for the speed with which a writer comes up with a problem. Here is the first paragraph I used in *Willow Hill*:

> Whenever there was a pause in dinner table conversation, Val glanced anxiously at the clock on the dining room wall. Plenty of time. The train from California wouldn't reach Willow Hill till after seven-thirty. More than an hour away and the minutes were dragging.

Again we have the thoughts of the main character, with promise of something interesting about to happen.

When I speak of action in the opening of a story, I don't mean the high moment of a football game, or a slugging match. Fast action openings of the physical type can be as dull as the dialogue opening. Until you find out about the people and care about them, you can't be interested in physical conflict. If you must use physical action at the very outset of your novel or story, use it to *characterize* at the same time. Who wins in such a conflict doesn't matter in the beginning—though whether a character (provided we have been introduced to him) can get out of a dangerous situation may matter very much. Impersonal action, impersonal danger, can be dull. Have you ever tuned in on a television car chase when you knew nothing about the situation leading up to it, or about the characters? You quickly switch to another station.

It is far better to present some plausible characters in immediate conflict because of something the main character wants to accomplish. The reader can determine his allegiance, and once having done so, will want to see his side win. When you feel that it is necessary to open the story or novel with only one character on the scene, show him doing something interesting before you allow him to think about it. But your task will be simplified if you have at least one other character—or even an animal—present for the character to talk to.

One of the best first pages of action I've come across lately is in a hard-punching boy's novel by Kin Platt called *Headman*. Here is the first paragraph:

> The silent fear came on slowly. Then it was rooted and part of him. The sun was blazing. Heat from the pavement sucked at his feet. Sweat crawled along his neck. The street was wide and empty but he needed more room. He lengthened his stride. The following footsteps shuffled relentlessly behind him.

Openings are fun to do, but they must be worked on and I have often thrown several away before I settle for one that seems right. Never be afraid to write for the wastebasket. You are not engraving on bronze when you put words on paper.

As you continue with the story, every early scene must leave the reader asking one or more questions. The moment curiosity is satisfied, interest drops. The technique of suspense consists in arousing the curiosity of the reader in the beginning. But curiosity alone is not enough. As soon as possible, it must be changed to anxiety as the reader wonders whether the main character can possibly win through to his goal.

Thus, there must be not only a main story problem which ties everything together, but a number of contributing, subsidiary but related problems, one or more in each succeeding scene. These your character may meet with either success or failure. Failure in itself carries the reader on to see what the character does to overcome the setback. If success comes too soon, interest may slacken, unless more problems and obstacles appear the moment one is solved.

None of this must be meaningless action. Even in a novel, what is happening must belong on the main track of the story. If you can dispense with any scene and never have it missed, then it doesn't belong in the first place.

If possible, avoid the use of flashback in your story. It *can* be used skillfully and effectively, but its dangers are many, and editors will like your work better if you don't use flashback in the short story. It is often used effectively in adult novels, but can be confusing to young readers, so use it with caution. If a flashback scene is very important, it may be wiser to start with that scene, presenting the flashback in direct action, instead of as something which happened before the start of your story. Then, with a skillful transition, you can connect it to the later scenes and get on with your story.

The danger of the flashback lies in loss of reader interest, when you switch from the present scene and must build up new concern for something which took place in the past. This loss is increased when, after finally getting your reader absorbed in the past scene, you must switch back to the present.

In *The Winter People* (an adult novel), I used one of my most effective openings:

> I was asleep, and then I was awake, listening. I could hear the snow hissing at the windows, hear the storm behind it and the rushing sound the wind made through the pine trees. But the sound that had wakened me was inside the house. A key had been slipped into a lock.

The heroine has been locked into her room, and her fear is built to a pitch as she begins to think back into the circumstances that brought her to this room and her present danger. Readers are led back into an interesting past they have been made curious about, and half the book is gone before the heroine is returned to her locked room. This was a very tricky flashback, and it could have infuriated my readers—but didn't seem to. In this case it worked.

When you come to the writing of your novel or story, you will find that transitions will play an important role. A scene has come to an end, and you must get characters and reader onto the next. This linkage between scenes may be of place or of time. The transition may also provide a brief point of rest for your readers. You cannot hold them at a constantly high pitch, so a marking of time, in which we move from one place to another or from one time to another, serves as a welcome release of tension, before we pick it up again. Sometimes, a transition consists of the movement of a character in time or space, or both. Sometimes he doesn't move at all, but time advances; other times, it is merely a reflective pause in which your main character thinks of what has just happened or is about to happen, or simply makes plans for the next action to be embarked upon, and while he is thinking, time passes.

The best way to learn how to handle transitions smoothly is to watch for them in your reading and collect samples that you copy into your notebook. To understand the effectiveness of a transition, you need to read what goes before and after.

Every new scene must grow out of the action that took place in the scene before, and in turn gives rise to the action which follows in the next scene. If at any point in the course of your writing you have a scene which does not grow naturally and directly out of a previous scene and move directly into the next one, you had better discard it entirely. No matter how delightful the incident may be on its own, no matter how fine the writing, if a scene is not tied to the main stem of your story plan, you will have to put it aside.

Sometimes in your writing, your imagination will present you with an entire scene, or a piece of action that you hadn't thought of ahead of time. Such "gifts" are not to be regarded lightly. Often the subconscious will have handed you something much better than what you had planned ahead of time. So write it as it comes; let it flow. Later, when you come to reread and revise, examine this unexpected gift and decide then whether it really belongs. Perhaps it opens up new possibilities for your story, or perhaps it goes down a side road, away from the direction you want to take. If the latter happens, throw it out, no matter how fond of it you have become.

The middle part of your story or novel is often the most difficult to write. After the first burst of enthusiasm, the imagination is apt to lag, and you may have to stop to give your story a chance to develop by methods I've already described. Making sure your main character has a purpose, a goal, in each scene is a good way to keep the interest high at this time. Let the character say to herself, "I am going to . . . ," and fill in that purpose for her, however large or small, and you will avoid middle-of-the-story lag.

Toward the end of the story or novel, obstacles must mount and disaster threaten, as we head toward the Black Moment just before dawn. If you can bring your main character to the very brink of disaster at this point, so the reader can't possibly guess how the story will end, you will ensure reader satisfaction at the conclusion. Readers like to be pleased and surprised. A twist in a direction never expected, but one which is still logical and could have been foretold, makes the most satisfying type of ending.

Whatever happens, don't skip the climax of your story. I have seen this occur again and again in beginners' manuscripts. The story builds toward its biggest, most dramatic scene, and then the writer, overcome by stage fright, paralysis, or mere laziness, skips to the next scene where everything is quiet again, and it is all over. Then we are told in retrospect how the problem was solved. Absolutely maddening and a sure way to disappoint your reader. The climax scene is the reader's reward for reading all the rest of your story. So give it all you've got.

Then, when you are through, *stop.* Don't go on and on explaining what has happened, or carry the characters through unnecessary additional scenes. Know when the drama is over, and try to wind it all up in a few graceful sentences. Sometimes, you can go back to your opening and find something appropriate to pick up again effectively in your closing paragraphs. Story and novel closings, like openings, must often be written several times in different ways before you hit on the right one. Again, study the story endings of successful writers. They are your best textbooks, right at your fingertips.

We cannot talk about putting a story together without some comment concerning style. Very often the young writer feels that style is something he must strive for by much polishing, by a deliberate choice of words, by various "literary" touches. It is true that most manuscripts can stand polishing, and that choice of words is important. But forget about being literary. Forget about impressing anyone with fine writing. Children are not interested in style. They are interested in *story*.

Aim for clarity, no matter what age you write for, and style need cause you no concern. It will develop by itself, and be uniquely yours, when you have put enough writing hours behind you.

Word books have been of great use to me. My *Roget's Thesaurus* has rescued me many times and aided me in making sure of the right word. No matter how excellent your vocabulary, it is not a good *working* vocabulary unless words come easily to your mind when you want them. I believe the years I spent using these books has improved my working vocabulary. I seldom need to refer to word books now, because my own word reservoir is well filled. Again, this is a matter of habit and training. Keep one of these books handy on your desk and reach for it the moment you are stumped.

The proof of your story pudding lies in presentation. The best story framework in the world can be spoiled by poor presentation. And sometimes very slipshod plots get by on presentation alone. Presentation does not mean style. It means how well you bring your characters alive, how cleverly you snare the reader's interest, how successful you are in achieving the illusion of reality. In short, how skill-fully you use all the cutting blades of that many-edged tool —technique.

The final writing of your story may prove difficult as you first try to apply the tool of technique. You remember one thing, only to forget another. You may despair of ever getting everything right at the same time, or even of getting a moderate number of things right at the same time, which is the best most of us can hope for. You will undoubtedly discover that whatever writing ease you may have known has gone from you, and you are now awkward and self-conscious. Don't let this disturb you. Revision will straighten out many of the things that are wrong, and as you write more and more stories, the ease will come.

During a planning period, I think a great deal about technique, but in the actual writing process, I have learned not to think of it at all. Practice in using any tool will enable you at last to use it without considering the tool itself, and then you will begin to get results. If you allow yourself to despair before that ease comes, you will have only yourself to blame for falling by the way.

11 | TAKING IT APART

"But I can't *rewrite*. Everything is fresh the first time. When I try to do it over, it takes all the life out of the story."

How many times I've heard novices say that! How many times I said it to myself when I was a beginning writer! Your subconscious whispers that you mustn't think of touching your little masterpiece; it is alive and sparkling now, even though unintelligent and unsympathetic critics may see a few chips around the edges. Better, far better, you tell yourself, to overlook those chipped places than to take the sparkle out of the jewel.

Unfortunately for the prospects of getting your story or novel published, the editor will see those chips immediately, and back your manuscript will come. It probably should never have been submitted in the first place. You might as well face the facts right now: Rewriting will undoubtedly take the life out of *you*, the writer, but not out of your story or novel.

Of course what is needed is not aimless revision, without benefit of direction or guidance. You must know what to look for. Again I suggest that you use the checklist in Chapter 5 and apply it carefully to your completed story or novel manuscript. This is important even though you will not be sure of all the answers; writers can never be completely satisfactory judges of their own work.

It is wiser not to revise immediately. When you reach the last page and write THE END, you are apt to experience a deceptive glow. If you sit down and read that story over then, you will probably be entranced with its virtues. You are too close to it, you have an affection for it, and one does not see with a sufficiently objective eye through the rosy haze of first love.

Of course you will want to send your manuscript off in the mail at once so that you can get a check back from the editor posthaste, but I suggest that you control this impulse and put the story away to "set."

Remember—it's the story that is to "set," not yourself. *You* are going to get busy immediately on a new story. When you have transferred your fickle affections to a new story idea, you will be in a far better position to go back and look at the old manuscript with a critical eye.

When I was writing short stories regularly, I worked out a system for myself. I always tried to keep "on ice" at least two stories that had as yet not gone into the mail. When I finished a third one, I put that on the bottom of the stack and took out the top one for a rereading. By that time the rosy haze had been dispelled and I could regard the story dispassionately. This is the only healthy attitude to have toward any story that has not seen print. After that story is in print and nothing further can be done to it, you may again be permitted a fatuous affection for it. Until that time, look only for its faults. Don't worry—they are there.

Above all, don't corner some unfortunate friend who knows nothing about writing and read it aloud to him. If he likes you, he'll probably like your story, whether it is any good or not. Just because your friends may read does not necessarily qualify them as critics.

Consider joining a writers' group, if you don't already belong to one. Read your manuscripts to them, and you will probably receive some healthy dashes of cold water. If your group pulls its punches and goes in for polite pats on the back, it might as well disband, for all the good it will do any of you.

If you can find a really competent critic, possibly a teacher or editor whose judgment you can trust (and they are rare indeed), let him read your story or novel manuscript. Don't argue and tell him he's all wrong and that he simply does not have the sensitivity to understand this delicate thing you are trying to achieve in your story. Go home and think about what he has said. Then get busy and rewrite your story or book manuscript.

Oh, of course, *you* are different. You can take criticism. You understand perfectly that nothing personal is implied. If your critic says your hero is a bit on the stupid side, it doesn't mean that *you* are stupid. You are not going to be upset in any way by what is said. You are asking for help because you really want it and you desire to make this story as perfect as you possibly can.

Don't fool yourself. You don't really mean a word of it. What you do mean is that you feel quite safe in asking for criticism because you know how good your story is and you are sure no one is going to say anything against it. What you really want is praise for your brain child.

When the critic rips your story or novel to pieces and leaves it a heap of rubble, the shock is going to send you into a state of collapse. You are not going to listen to a word of it with your mind—you are going to take the whole thing full force with your emotions. You are going to be crushed, wounded, left bleeding and despairing. All your high hopes have died, your dreams have been dispelled. How *could* this person whom you so trusted prove to be such a brute and hurt you so much? Why, now you don't even feel like writing any more. Your career has been blasted. You'll show him what he's done to you. Then he'll feel sorry.

Don't fool yourself; he won't. He'll merely look at you coldly, dust off his hands and walk away. And next time he'll know better. When you go to him for help (as you undoubtedly will), he'll regard you sadly and shake his head. After all, he has his own sensitivities, and he'd rather keep you as a friend (goodness knows why!) than so alienate you with his criticism of your story manuscript.

You may, if you like, disregard everything else I've told you in this book, but listen to me, please, on this. Good stories are not written. They are *re*written.

So you will have to set about growing callouses in the right places. Emotion is something which has a very definite place in your story, but it has no place at all in the way in which you receive criticism. Take it for granted that there will be plenty wrong with your story. Perfection is all too rare. Many stories that get published have lots wrong with them and could be improved still further. See to it that revision improves your story to the limit of your ability before you send it out. Listen to your critics *with your mind,* weigh and consider, and never, never argue. If in the final judgment you disagree, that is your affair. But don't wrangle over anything they tell you. Store it away and consider it soberly.

Revision is an unpleasant, grubby job. Until you learn how, it can be dull, boring, and hateful. But it is perhaps the most important part of writing. Revision may take the life out of a writer. All the freshness, all the adventure, all the excitement of meeting new characters appears to be gone, and you may have a deep loathing for every word you write during revision. Oddly enough, your feeling on this does not seem to show in the final version. The passages which were written with sweat and blood and anger very often sound much better than those you left as they were first written.

Let me tell you something else—something that may both comfort and depress you. Writing doesn't necessarily get any easier for the experienced author of many stories and books. Words may come more easily, and certain aspects become more understandable, but professional writers are also capable of bad writing in their first drafts.

Don't be one of those writers who gives up when everything goes wrong. I can think of several successful writers who were being published regularly, then happened to turn out a bad manuscript—and quit. They haven't been heard from since, simply because they lacked the courage and determination to rewrite it. It does take courage and a blind sort of determination to start over—perhaps *all* over. Yet, sometimes this has to be done.

The more I learn about writing, the more revision I seem to do. A friend who is a beginning writer visited me recently and showed an interest in looking through some of my old manuscripts. I liked her comment: "Why, they look just as bad as my manuscripts, and that makes me feel better!" A manuscript *should* look bad before the final typing.

Before you take your fiction manuscript to a critic or send it to an editor, there is a last checklist you can run through that may help:

1. Is the problem clear? Is it one which will interest the age for which your story is intended?

2. Are your characters individualized? Are they consistent? Are the main character and his problem presented sympathetically?

3. What point are you trying to make, and did you make it?

4. Is there a subsidiary problem in every scene, and a carry-over of interest to the next scene?

5. Is there a scene which could be omitted from the story and not be missed?

6. Is your climax emotionally satisfying?

7. What about logic and motivation? Do these ring true, or were you trying to force some action to suit your own purposes?

These last two are especially important. If you have portrayed your leading character in a certain way, there are some things it would be illogical to have him do. He must stay *in character* all the way through. His every move must be properly motivated.

Learn to listen to the inner voice that will whisper to you and question certain points in your story. Often it is not a very insistent voice, and you may brush it aside because you want to think everything is all right and can "get by" on this score. I have learned that if there is so much as a hint of doubt, I'd better check into the matter thoroughly and do a little revision at that point. Otherwise, I usually find to my regret that this is the very angle some critic leaps upon and rips to shreds.

There is no easy road to getting a story right. But in the long run you will find that grubbing at this point pays.

12 | SPECIALIZATION

It is quite likely that after you have experimented for a while with the writing of various types of fiction, you will want to narrow the field down and specialize in one or two particular types. You will decide whether you want to write for boys or girls, whether you want to write about the modern scene or use historical material, whether you want to write for the teens, the in-between age, or for younger children. In these groups there may be still further specialization.

Your best guide, when you decide upon some special field, is to go to the children's room of any library and stock up on books in that field. Read them in quantity, until you know them well enough to compare the merits of different writers, and to recognize their flaws. Do this whether you intend to write books or not. Talk to children's librarians and find out what the youngsters themselves think. Why do the books by one author wear out and need replacing in a comparatively short period, while the books of another sit untouched on the shelves? You can find out these things best by doing some research of your own, and by reading books written for the age you want to write for. Steep yourself in what is being written in that field. In that way, too, you can learn what has been written over and over, so many times that you had better avoid it; you might discover a fresh slant. This, of course, applies to the magazine field as well. Read copies of the magazines for which you want to write so that you will know what the editors are buying.

Let's take a brief look at a few special fields.

FANTASY

If you intend to write for young children, it is possible that you will be attracted first of all to writing fantasy. The advice I must give you at this point is to approach with caution.

It isn't that children do not care for stories of make-believe. Most children love them. And it isn't that editors are not delighted to publish really good stories of this kind. The difficulty lies in the fact that fantasy is the easiest thing of all to write badly, and the most difficult to write well.

Editors' desks overflow with tales of "Little Miss Moon-beam," or "The Unhappy Pumpkin Seed," or "The Little Lost Cloud." The chances are good that if you write that sort of thing, your manuscript won't be read past the first page. In fact, the editor will probably pull your story half-way out of the envelope, say, "Oh, another one!" and send it straight back to you. If you are trying to break into the juvenile field, I assure you, fantasy is no Open Sesame. You'll need unusual talent, wisdom, a good sense of humor, and an expert way with words before you can turn out anything outstanding in this field.

If you do write fantasy, try to avoid the trite, the done-to-death. Page through the picture books in your library for overused themes. Inanimate objects that think and talk may still appear in storybooks for the very young, but if you follow this course, you will need to be original, because this kind of fantasy has already been done so often.

The situation is not nearly so discouraging now as it was some years ago. In the last ten years or so there has been a noteworthy resurgence of fantasy. We have emerged from the all-must-be-real period with its tendency to belittle make-believe. Today bookstores are piled high with excellent books of fantasy. There are modern "classics" in-the-making: Maurice Sendak's *Where the Wild Things Are,* Madeleine L'Engle's *A Wrinkle in Time,* Ursula K. Le Guin's Earthsea Trilogy and all the Tolkien books are increasingly popular with readers of various ages. New writers are making their reputation in the fantasy field.

Certainly this trend is a healthy one. The mind and imagination of the young reader need to be encouraged to soar and develop. Among the excellent fantasy titles currently available are: C. S. Lewis' *The Lion, the Witch and the Wardrobe* and the six sequels that make up the Chronicles of Narnia; Edward Eager's humorous and expertly plotted novels which bridge the thin line between fantasy and reality, *Half Magic, Magic by the Lake, Seven-Day Magic, Magic or Not?,* and *The Well-Wisher;* Rumer Godden's doll stories—*Impunity Jane, The Dolls' House, Home Is the Sailor,* and *Miss Happiness and Miss Flower;* Kenneth Grahame's durable *Wind in the Willows* and *The Reluctant Dragon;* Hugh Lofting's Dr. Dolittle novels; a large number of humorous fantasy stories with kind and peculiar old ladies with magical powers as main characters, such as Betty MacDonald's Mrs. Piggle-Wiggle books, Ellen MacGregor's novels about Miss Pickerell, and P. L. Travers's Mary Poppins books. There are also superb contemporary evocations in classical fairy tale style: James Thurber's *Many Moons* and *The 13 Clocks;* Phyllis McGinley's *The Plain Princess;* and many fine books about "little people," of which the most popular and widely read have been Mary Norton's *The Borrowers* and its several sequels. Many contemporary authors of successful fantasy have been at least in part influenced by the works of E. Nesbit, whose tales of the power of magic and imagination are at their best in the author's *The Enchanted Castle* (1906) and as popular today as L. Frank Baum's *The Wonderful Wizard of Oz* (1900).

An excellent example of fantasy combined with the everyday world is William MacKellar's amusing *Alfie and Me and the Ghost of Peter Stuyvesant,* read by 8 to 12's.

ANIMAL STORIES

Stories or novels about animals, often related to fantasy, are perennial favorites with young people. It used to be the convention in this field that if your animals talk, they should talk only among themselves and not to the human beings in the story. This rule, however, has been broken successfully many times, but everything depends on how well you do it.

Stories of make-believe often seem to be more acceptable when they deal with animals than when they are about people, though any mixture of the two is possible.

There do not appear to be any taboos on the type of animal or creature you write about. If you can make Sammy Snake or Timothy Turtle interesting enough, you needn't feel limited to writing about more cuddly animals. Margaret Bloy Graham has made *Benjy the Barking Bird* quite whimsically believable. Pets are, of course, acceptable in all kinds of children's stories and can often help move your plot along.

The educational factor may also work to the writer's advantage. If you know a great deal about the habits of some particular animal, stories about it will probably be welcomed by parents and teachers. You may even become another Felix Salten and give the world a *Bambi*.

Watership Down by Richard Adams was written originally for children and has become a best seller for all readers. Robert Lawson's *Rabbit Hill* and *The Tough*

Winter succeed in part because the author has combined his love of the Connecticut countryside with a childlike insight into the mischief of small animals in woods and fields. The brief, easy-to-read, but disarmingly profound *Little Bear* books by Else Minarik, and Russell Hoban's stories about Frances the badger deal with such childhood emotions as sibling rivalry (*A Baby Sister for Frances*), loneliness (*Best Friends for Frances*), fear of the dark (*Bedtime for Frances*), and food fetishes (*Bread and Jam for Frances*), and are typical of the way animals may be used by writers to point up human weaknesses and strengths. The successful author of animal fantasy for children captures the reader's interest and imagination and often relates highly amusing and even moral tales filled with important truths that might make the child reader uncomfortable if presented in realistic terms involving human characters. One of the most stunning achievements of this kind is E. B. White's modern classic, *Charlotte's Web,* a novel universally popular with children, which deals uncompromisingly but not depressingly with the fear of death. While this book may be read and appreciated at several levels, even very young children unconsciously understand the basic themes of fear and death which pervade this landmark of children's literature. No writer who intends to employ animals as examples of human experience and personality should miss reading White's unforgettable story of Wilbur the pig and his loyal friend and mentor, Charlotte the spider.

Biting satire and hilarious humor are found in Margery Sharp's ultrasophisticated *The Rescuers* novels. These prove the elusive appeal and versatility of mice, and illustrate again that the writer of animal stories may comment to young people on the world and human nature in terms that might be unacceptable to readers in a realistic setting.

The insatiable demand of youngsters for animal books of

all types has produced a literary genre that is a hybrid of fact and fiction, a style that reads like a novel or story but contains authentic factual and scientific information. Especially successful with this type of book have been Alice Goudey (*Here Come the Bears, Here Come the Bees,* etc.), Jean George (*The Moon of the Salamanders, The Moon of the Mountain Lions,* etc.), and Robert McClung (*Buzztail, Black Jack, Redbird,* etc.). Other authors have specialized with repeated success in writing realistic fiction about a particular kind of animal. Writers such as C. W. Anderson, Walter Farley, and Marguerite Henry, for instance, have a wide audience for their horse stories.

In considering fantasy and animal stories, I warn you again to avoid what I've come to call the "journey story" —in which floating dandelion fuzz or a baby bear starts out to see the world. He (it) visits here, makes certain encounters there, and then goes on to the next place. This continues through the book, until the "traveler" usually winds up finding that home is best. This story has been published countless times, but I feel certain that it would be rejected by editors today. The pattern is not only trite; it is also a mere stringing together of incidents, lacking any real plot. Stay away from it.

HISTORICAL

If you have a natural flair for writing about the past, historical fiction is a good field for you to specialize in. You may write about any period or phase of history that appeals to you—all of time and the entire world are yours to choose from. But first you must steep yourself in the country or setting and period you plan to write about until you feel as if you had lived in that time or place.

Whether aimed at the picture book age or the teens, the historical story or novel has been regarded with a kindly eye by editors and librarians. These stories are often promoted for their "educational" value, and, sad to say, this factor has weighed so heavily in their favor that much rather dull historical fiction has been published and inflicted upon young readers.

Period fiction may be hard to sell at present; nonfiction is taking over in the historical field, and if you like history and want to base what you write on actual happenings, you stand a better chance writing nonfiction. But even here fiction techniques should be used to build interest.

Two of my most durable teen-age novels which have stayed in print over the years were based on historical fact. *Step to the Music* dealt with the Civil War years, showing actual happenings on Staten Island. *The Fire and the Gold* presented the aftermath of the San Francisco earthquake and fire, and the spirit of the people as they started to rebuild. After writing these two books for young people, I used the same backgrounds and historical facts for my adult novels, *The Quicksilver Pool* and *The Trembling Hills*, though the stories and characters are totally different.

Here are a few examples of period novels that show signs of lasting and continuing to appeal to readers: Patricia Beatty has a growing reputation for her novels about the settling of Washington and Oregon and the concurrent struggle for women's rights, as in her *Hail Columbia*. Carol Brink's *Caddie Woodlawn* is the best known of several fine novels about the pioneer struggle in the Western half of the United States. So, too, of course, are the semi-autobiographical *Little House* novels of Laura Ingalls Wilder. Clyde Bulla has written a large number of shorter, relatively easy-to-read historical novels about American Indians, the pioneer life, medieval Britain, and the Vikings. Sydney Taylor, in her *All-of-a-Kind* books, has evoked urban life in turn-of-the-century America. Such novels as *The Door in the*

Wall, about Europe in the Middle Ages, *Elin's Amerika,* about the seventeenth-century settlement of Delaware, and *Thee, Hannah!,* which relates the Quaker dilemma during the Civil War, illustrate Marguerite de Angeli's wide-ranging mastery of the historical novel for the eight- to sixteen-year-old. William Steele has a huge audience among adventure-seeking youngsters who avidly read his novels set in America's past, among them, *Flaming Arrows* and *The Perilous Road.* Walter Edmonds has written about the French and Indian War (*The Matchlock Gun*) and the Civil War from the viewpoint of North and South (*Cadmus Henry*). The best historical novel written for young people about the titanic struggle of the War Between the States may be Irene Hunt's *Across Five Aprils,* a deeply moving and realistic account of the war's impact on an Illinois farm family. And Esther Forbes's novel *Johnny Tremain* ranks with the finest juvenile historical accounts of the Revolutionary War. While Robert Lawson's *Ben and Me* and *Mr. Revere and I* are basically fantasies, they impart a great deal of accurate historical information and flavor, using an amusing and clever literary technique.

One successful device used in writing this type of story or novel is making the characters speak as they do today. Get the flavor of the time into your dialogue, but avoid stiffness and formality. Don't make the characters speak exactly in the words they might have used at the time in history when your story takes place. Of course you must avoid modern slang or the result will be jarring. Get to know your characters as if they were youngsters who live on your block, rather than figures who belong in the past. They must be made very real and sympathetic to young people today. The more strange and foreign the names of your people, the more convincing your characterization must be.

I have often been asked how to present historical facts in such fiction, since the group of characters acting out the story may not be aware of the larger events of history going on about them. I had to solve this problem in my novel *Step to the Music,* where certain battles and events of the Civil War had to be mentioned in order to give the reader a feeling of what was happening, even though my heroine might not have been aware of those occurrences. I used the device of opening certain chapters with the omniscient viewpoint rather than my heroine's. Here is an example:

> June was hot and long and during its course Staten Island burst into a buzzing place of military camps. Uniforms were to be seen everywhere and the island began to experience its first trouble with undisciplined soldiers. The *Gazette* carried accounts of drunken assaults on the street, thievery, and vandalism. The old sleepy days were gone and roads bore the new ruts of cannon wheels, the hoof marks of cavalry. Because of the camps, visitors poured in by the hundreds, and on Sunday dust hung like a pall over roads where loaded stages rolled.

In the next paragraph, I slipped back into the heroine's viewpoint and stayed there for the rest of the chapter. Using this technique will also provide time transitions and even cover distant events. But don't weave back and forth within one chapter or you will confuse the reader.

THE MODERN AMERICAN STORY

Modern American fiction is the most popular category of all. Almost anything goes, the old taboos are off, and there are books that deal with almost any youth problem you can imagine—especially at the teen-age level. Drugs, sex, alcohol, illegitimate babies, crime, all possible family situations, homosexuality—anything and everything can be discussed openly and with all the honesty writers can bring to the task.

Paul Zindel, Judy Blume, Harry and Norma Mazer, and others are among those writing fiction on these "real" subjects.

However, there are many books in this category—particularly those for younger readers—that are realistic but somewhat less grim than those for the teen-age reader.

The realistic novel for young people today is dominated by a number of highly competent authors. Lois Lenski, for instance, has built a solid reputation with her regional novels about contrasting American life styles (*Strawberry Girl, Prairie School*, etc.). Jean Little writes moving novels about previously "forbidden" themes, like death, cerebral palsy, and the retarded child aimed at the audience of middle and later childhood. Beverly Cleary writes very funny, only slightly larger-than-life novels about lively, enthusiastic, and mischievous youngsters, such as *Henry Huggins, Ellen Tebbits,* and *Otis Spofford.* E. L. Konigsburg has captured the agonies and ecstasies of middle-class suburban life in such novels as *From the Mixed-up Files of Mrs. Basil E. Frankweiler* and *About B'nai Bagels.* Keith Robertson has chronicled the drive of enterprising youth in his *Henry Reed, Inc., Henry Reed's Baby-Sitting Service,* etc. In the Melendy family series of novels, beginning with *The Saturdays,* Elizabeth Enright has written about how well brothers and sisters can get along and how much they mean to each other. Louise Fitzhugh's *Harriet the Spy,* a funny and compassionate novel of a terrifying sixth-grader whose caustic personality made her an outcast among her peers, has, after creating a great deal of controversy, won a lasting place. Eleanor Estes's *The Hundred Dresses* effectively portrays the sufferings of those who are different, with a story of the loneliness that drives a little girl into a world of daydreams. Harry Mazer in *Snowbound* has told a gripping, up-to-the-minute story of two children who detest each other, are stranded in a blizzard in a stalled car, and must struggle to stay alive.

But Carolyn Haywood is outstanding among children's novelists in her ability to capture the mind and perception of the child and to create a "real" world. Her style is simple and direct; her vocabulary choice and precise; her sentence structure clear; and her characterizations and settings economically and brilliantly evoked. She relates children's everyday home and school experiences with understanding and insight. Some of her best titles include *Betsy's Little Star, Betsy and Billy, Back to School with Betsy, Little Eddie, Penny and Peter, Snowbound with Betsy* and *"C" Is for Cupcake.*

ETHNIC FICTION

Racial themes are particularly important, since America contains a very large intermixture of ethnic groups. At the time when I began writing for young people there was very little available in this field—particularly when it came to books that dealt honestly with black Americans.

Florence Crannell Means was one of the pioneers in writing about problems of race, and her books, *Shuttered Windows, Great Day in the Morning,* as well as those dealing with Indian problems, are still remembered as breaking the way for the writers who were to follow. Her courageous novel, *The Moved-Outers,* is a classic story of the sad treatment of Japanese-Americans during World War II.

Another pioneer whose books should not be forgotten is John Tunis. In the sports field he often dealt with the problems of prejudice, and there are many adults today who grew up with his books and were perhaps changed a little in their thinking because of them.

It is a far cry from the John Tunis who dared to use "damn" in one of his books thirty years ago, to Kin Platt's

Headman, which hardly misses a four-letter word. Yet I think John Tunis might approve of this powerful, hard-punching novel, which deals with white, black, and Chicano gangs in Los Angeles.

My own *Willow Hill,* published in 1947, is still in print, and deals with prejudice in a midwestern high school. In that book the word "Negro" is used all the way through, since "black" would have been considered a taboo word.

There have sometimes been objections to authors who write from ethnic viewpoints other than their own, stemming from the feeling that if a writer doesn't belong by birth to the group he (or she) writes about, he cannot possibly understand the problems of these people. I don't agree. While we certainly need more books by the members of all ethnic groups, a writer of any ethnic background, as long as he has knowledge and imagination, can write a good "ethnic" book. Those who write about ancient history were never there. I have never murdered anyone, yet I have written about characters in my adult books who are motivated to kill—and it is possible to understand such motivation and portray it convincingly in a novel or short story. If you can write with understanding about Eskimos or Fiji Islanders and want to, do it! And I don't mind at all if Eskimos and Fiji Islanders write about me, provided they have the knowledge and understanding to do so.

Books that deal with racial, religious, or sexual bigotry in the most indirect, understated, or casual manner are probably the most effective in their impact on the reader. In Ezra Jack Keats's *The Snowy Day,* the fact that the characters were black drew positive reaction simply because that fact was accepted from the outset, and no mention was or needed to be paid to it. Books like those by Keats have made an enormous contribution to interracial and religious understanding. It is important to bear in mind in writing about minority groups that while differences may be explicitly stated and be crucial to the plot, theme, or flavor of the story, they are most disarming to the reader when presented in a matter-of-fact, unselfconscious and understated way.

Ethnic themes in books for young people have had a strong influence on changing views in our society; the concepts and attitudes of countless citizens have undoubtedly been affected by their juvenile reading experiences. Many of the early novels of Lois Lenski (*Cotton in My Sack*), Doris Gates (*Little Vic, Blue Willow*), and Marguerite de Angeli (*Bright April*) offer original and enriching insights into the cultural traditions of the American Negro.

Many fine novels relating the adventures of children who came to America from Europe as pioneers or as immigrants, as rural or urban settlers, have transmitted to young readers abundant information about specific ethnic patterns of behavior, traditions, customs, and ethical values. Leo Politi has effectively depicted the life style of Mexicans in the United States (*Pedro and the Nicest Gift, The Angel of Olvera Street*); of Chinese in the United States (*Moy Moy*); and of Americans in Italy (*Little Leo*). Valenti Angelo's *The Bells of Bleeker Street* has become a classic juvenile novel of the urban Italian ghetto around the time of World War II; Mildred Walter's *Lillie of Watts* an unforgettable portrait of a young girl growing up in the black neighborhood of Los Angeles; and Jennie Lindquist's *The Golden Name Day* and *The Little Silver House* have become staple fiction narratives about the Swedish traditions preserved in New England. Yoshiko Uchida's *The Promised Year* relates the sharp contrasts in Japanese and American values when a Japanese girl comes to California for a year's visit, and Norma Simon's *Ruthie* deals with the clash between orthodox and reformed Jewish values and patterns.

Segregation in education has been effectively treated in

Betty Baum's *Patricia Crosses Town* and most memorably in Natalie Carlson's *The Empty Schoolhouse*. Of Pura Belpré's several books about the Puerto Rican life style and culture, *Santiago* is one of the best concerning the problems of Puerto Rican communities in New York City. Robert Burch's books, such as *Joey's Cat* and *D.J.'s Worst Enemy*, are faithful depictions of black and white interrelationships in rural Georgia. Emily Neville's *Berries Goodman, It's Like This, Cat* and *The Seventeenth-Street Gang* are noteworthy examples of good stories set against ethnically heterogeneous urban neighborhoods. Helen Coutant's bittersweet *First Snow* and Paige Dixon's strongly antiwar *Promises to Keep* both relate the experiences of Vietnamese refugees transported to New England. Virginia Hamilton's *M.C. Higgins, the Great*, Bette Greene's *Philip Hall Likes Me, I Reckon Maybe* and Nicholasa Mohr's *Nilda* are highly effective portraits of the varieties of Negro and Puerto Rican life without excessive ethnic self-consciousness.

STORIES OF FOREIGN LANDS

Novels with foreign backgrounds, settings, and characters are probably more in demand by teachers and librarians than by the children themselves, but there is a need for them.

If you know enough about a foreign country to write about it through the eyes of those who live there, that is fine. If not, however, there is a device you can use that will serve you well. I have written a great many books set in other countries, both for young people and for adults, and in every case I write from the viewpoint of an American *visitor*. This viewpoint is my own, and I can use my knowledge (and my ignorance) to good effect. There is also an appeal to the young reader when he can follow a character with whom he feels empathy, into a foreign setting.

Patricia Wrightson has written a number of novels set in various parts of Australia dealing with subjects ranging from the problems of the mentally handicapped (*A Racehorse for Andy*), to exciting science fiction happenings near Sydney (*Down to Earth*). Maia Wojciechowska's *Shadow of a Bull* and Eva-Lis Wuorio's *Save Alice!* are presented with vivid images of Spain. Claire Bishop has written successfully about Switzerland (*All Alone*) and France (*Pancakes—Paris* and *Twenty and Ten*); L. M. Boston's *Green Knowe* books provide an accurate account of English country life; India is brought to life in Shirley Arora's *What Then, Raman?*, Louise Rankin's *Daughter of the Mountains,* and dozens of Kipling's stories. Pearl Buck's *The Big Wave* is an American's timeless evocation of Japanese village life. Elizabeth Coatsworth's novels use as settings Japan (*The Cat Who Went to Heaven*), France (*The Fair American*), and mysterious Morocco (*The White Horse*). Meindert DeJong writes with equal mastery of China (*The House of Sixty Fathers*) and the Netherlands (*The Wheel on the School*). Kate Seredy's books set in Hungary are still widely read; *The Good Master* is probably her most popular. Anico Surany (*Monsieur Jolicoeur's Umbrella*) and Morna Stuart (*Marassa and Midnight*) have been specializing in writing stories of Central and South American cultures, and Ruth Tooze has written a number of books set in Southeast Asia, one of the best of which is *Silver from the Sea,* about the children of Vietnam.

A word should be said about the use of dialect in writing about other countries and communities. To accomplish the flavor of a language, use idiom rather than dialect. Transpose the order of your words, rearrange sentence structure, use phraseology common to the group or region about which you are writing, but *don't* use unusual contractions, incorrect grammar, odd spellings, and the like. They are hard on the eye and tend to discourage most young readers from finishing a story. Readers familiar with a particular foreign country and its peoples may read the story easily because they know how your odd spellings really sound when spoken correctly. But the outsider has no idea and may spend so much time trying to figure out what your character is saying that the effect of your story may be completely wasted.

Here is an example of idiom in dialogue from William MacKellar's classic, *Wee Joseph*.

> "Aye, it's a grand dog he is for certain, Mr. Blaikie," he agreed. "Will you look at the rare markings on him? I'm thinking there will not be many like him in these parts."

Only a few lines, but we have been given the flavor of the Scottish tongue.

In your own reading watch for this use of idiom, learn to listen to and make notes of dialect from real-life conversations of foreign people; take note of turns of phrase, inflections, special vocabulary and word placement or unusual usage, as well as voice modulations.

SCIENCE FICTION

There has been a remarkable resurgence of science fiction in the past few years. Robert Heinlein, Isaac Asimov, Arthur C. Clarke, and many others have long been writing top-quality science fiction, but the demand for it is growing. Science fiction, it should be noted, is one of those categories that seems to cut across every age division! Quite young people avidly read and enjoy so-called adult science fiction novels and stories (just as many adults are devoted to fantasy originally designated as "juvenile"; Ursula Le Guin's Earth-sea Trilogy is an excellent example). In any case, it is a popular field worth looking into if you have knowledge and liking for this kind of imaginative writing. There is probably more emphasis on authentic science these days than ever before, and perhaps real science is fantastic enough.

Madeleine L'Engle's *A Wrinkle in Time* has become a modern classic in this field, and there are other writers widely read today, such as Eleanor Cameron (*Time and Mr. Bass*), Jay Williams (Danny Dunn books), and Alexander Key (*Escape to Witch Mountain* and *The Forgotten Door*), Oliver Butterworth (*The Enormous Egg*), and Louis Slobodkin, whose many amusing science fiction tales include *The Space Ship Under the Apple Tree*.

An unusual and outstanding example of modern science fiction is Norma Mazer's novel for teen-age girls, *Saturday the Twelfth of October*.

GENERAL COMMENTS

Fiction, in the past, used to be broken down into such categories as sports, adventure, mystery, school, hobby, vocations, romance, etc. The boundaries between these are less rigid nowadays than they used to be, and categories can blur and intermingle—which is all to the good. "Relevance" is probably the key word with editors today, and that can cover almost anything that is going on in the world.

One important trend that every writer should be aware of is the avoidance of sexism in children's books. Perhaps the objections have at times been a bit excessive, but it may require excessive reactions to jar us into awareness so that we can take a new look at something we have never had challenged before.

Many otherwise excellent juvenile titles have been justly criticized for their sexist views of life and the rigid sex-defined roles they have portrayed to readers at impressionable ages. Must reading for any juvenile author who wishes to avoid the pitfalls of sex-role stereotyping is *Free to Be You and Me,* Marlo Thomas's collaboration with Carole Hart, Gloria Steinem, and others. Tomboys still abound in juvenile fiction but with far less apology, as in Julia First's *Flat on My Face* and Constance Greene's *Isabelle the Itch,* but boy characters who prefer activities traditionally associated with girls still appear to be taboo. Perhaps Eve Merriam, in her *Boys and Girls, Girls and Boys,* and Judith Viorst, in *Rosie and Michael,* have come closest to handling this difficult theme with honesty and understanding.

Barriers are not only down, but it is essential to recognize there are new role models for male and female characters. In today's novels and stories for young readers, Mother can run a tractor, a boy can cook, anyone can be a jockey or run a train. At the same time, if I want to have the mother in a story or novel make cookies and in "typical" style keep house and prepare meals for the family, I think that's all right, too! Just be aware of the effect your use of conventional characters will have on your readers.

If you want to write for children, you should become familiar with *The Horn Book Magazine* and *School Library Journal.* These periodicals deal entirely with children's books. They contain articles written by experts in the field and will keep you abreast of the newest trends and views, as well as suggest good books for you to read.

A few last words to close a chapter that is especially concerned with content. Relevance is fine, but not all books have to deal with a Message in capital letters. We must never lose sight of the fact that reading first of all should be fun. Sometimes it can be fun to cry, fun to be frightened in the pages of a novel. But not all fiction needs to be stark and grim. Bear in mind that there is truth in the beautiful as well as in the ugly. While writers and readers must face reality to grow and to change what is wrong, sometimes everyone needs to escape into make-believe for rest and relief.

When readers write to tell me that they couldn't put down one of my books until the end, I feel I have achieved my purpose. Write your stories and novels to interest and entertain, as well as to inform. Reading should be a lifetime's pleasure.

13 | THE NOVEL

It is much more fun for me to write novels than to write short stories. The grueling part of any writing is working out the plan. That is the difficult, the creative part. True, it takes longer to plot a novel than it does to plot a short story, but once you have the plot for your book worked out, your path is fairly simple. Your work schedule stretches ahead of you for several months, and you know exactly where the story is going. When you are in the process of writing a novel, you don't have to think up a new plot every few days, as you must when you are writing short stories.

Another obvious point in favor of writing book-length fiction is the fact that there is a very small market for short stories these days. They are hard to sell. The paperback market for young people is opening up and will be hungrier than ever for novels for children and "young adults," though at present there are more reprints than originals in the young people's paperback field. So look toward writing book-length fiction eventually, but do your wastebasket practice in the short story field.

As I've said before, the short story is the more difficult, but it's the best form in which to experiment. The first attempt, however, to change from short story writing to novel writing may be a little frightening.

Some writers never succeed in the book field because they

allow the size of the task to frighten them off. They may start a book, even two or three books, but somehow they never get around to finishing them. The prospect of looking 60,000 words or more in the eye leaves them fearful of their ability to complete the job.

Because of the cost of paper and printing today, publishers are happier with shorter book lengths, and you need not think that you must write to a set goal of 60,000 words or so. Use the wordage your novel needs and cut later, if necessary. I find it easier for me to write it short from the outset. A careful examination of books on library shelves will show you the current requirements of various publishers, as will market lists of publishers who are looking for juvenile fiction.

When you first start writing book-length fiction, whatever the number of pages, any kind of book for older children may seem frighteningly long. If length worries you, just think of it one chapter at a time. Suppose your chapters run 3,000 words each (not an absolute figure), and you plan to write twenty chapters. If you write one chapter a week for twenty weeks, you will have a book. That's a slow rate of speed and not at all alarming—yet it will result in a book.

I am going to tell you how I work out a book-length novel. Because this is *my* way, I like it, but remember that no one writer's way is *the* way. There are probably as many methods of working as there are writers, and it is best to find the way most comfortable for you. The house-building analogy is all very well as far as it goes, but it is not a perfect analogy. The building of a house is a more or less exact technique, manual and mechanical. The writing of a story or a novel is mental, emotional, psychological; a great deal of blueprinting and technical planning may be done, but in the final reckoning, it is a thing of the mind and the emotions. Try to the best of your ability to condition your-self in the beginning to sensible, efficient working habits, but if any plan restricts *you,* if the effort to fit yourself to someone else's working method results in inhibiting your imagination—you must go your own way and listen to your own voices.

This is perhaps a dangerous thing to say, because it will be to your greatest advantage if you *do* discipline yourself to accepting certain edicts of technique. I am not anxious to offer an easy excuse to the young writer who feels he knows it all, when he has learned very little about putting a good novel or story together. It may be a temptation to say, "Ah, but these irksome matters are restricting my creative pro-cesses and I'll be better off to go my own way." Don't say that too quickly if you want to sell what you write. But once you have learned the fundamentals of telling a good story, then work out your own method of getting that story written. Find out how other writers work. Adapt what you can from their methods and discard whatever seems to restrain you too greatly.

These days, when all is going smoothly, I am able to write one adult suspense novel, and one young people's mystery in a year. The adult book takes about eight months, and the much shorter juvenile about four. The limits to how long I work on each are never fixed. Each book must have whatever time *it* requires. I do try, however, to plan a working schedule ahead, allowing (for a juvenile) about one month for planning, two months for writing, and one month for revision and typing. With each book, the sched-ule can change, and I try to keep flexible, while still, when-ever possible, working within the four-month limit.

The planning of a book, though lengthier and more complicated, is not so very different from the planning of a short story. You are going to have more time to develop characters, you are going to bring in many more situations and scenes, but you will do a great many of the same things you did in the shorter length.

When I first began to write novels, my system for planning book-length fiction was decidedly a hodgepodge. It consisted of envelopes, loose pages, scraps of paper. My organization was nil, and I wasted a prodigious amount of time and energy and gave little thought to devices that would increase my creative flow. When I was working on a novel, I was often stumped, lost in a sea of unclassified notes, and used my time inefficiently.

Then I moved from Chicago to New York and started to teach juvenile writing at New York University. My students began to ask embarrassing questions about how *I* wrote a book. I couldn't bear to tell them and couldn't have explained my "system" anyway. So I sat down at the start of a new book I planned to write and developed a system of organizing my material. I decided that I would first see whether this worked for me, and if it did, I would present it to my classes.

It worked so well that I have used it ever since, letting it grow and improve. Now when I am about to begin a new book my first step is to clear all the old pages of my last piece of fiction from my notebook, put in clean paper under all the headings, and start out fresh. This same notebook has by this time given birth to at least fifty of my books, and I have become attached to it in all its shabbiness. A few years ago, I did dress it up by removing the worn and soiled divider pages, putting in new, bright-colored ones, labeled with new tabs that hadn't been smudged with fingerprints. All good for the morale.

What I want to give you now are the headings I use for my notebook, with some discussion of each section. First, a word about the physical characteristics of this notebook.

Pages 5½ x 8½ seem a comfortable size to me. In my last rehabilitation of the notebook, I bought colored construction paper from a stationery store and cut it into the dividers I wanted. I also bought linen tabs and labeled them in red ink—on both sides, since I move both ways in using the notebook. Be sure your notebook has large rings, since otherwise it won't hold enough paper and you'll find yourself crowded. Mine is actually made of leather, dating back to the days before plastic.

If you are a born writer, all this preparation will fascinate you and help to make you feel good about writing a book. While some women stand in front of dress shop windows, studying styles, my favorite windows are always those of stationery stores.

Now for the headings on those tabs.

CALENDAR

This is my first section, and the first page is headed WORK CALENDAR, and dated with the year. Later, I'll write in the title of the book, when I have it, as these pages will eventually be put away in an envelope, to be preserved. It's surprising how many times you may want to look back at old work records.

Near the top of this first page I write *Plotting Begun, Plotting Finished,* with spaces for entering dates. Next comes *Started Writing* and *Finished Writing,* again with spaces for dates. I will also want a record of when I started and finished the revision, started and finished the typing, and when I sent off the manuscript. Underneath all this, I write a rough "measurement" to guide me, such as:

15 chapters, 12 pages each = 180 pp.

This gives me a goal to work toward, though each of my chapters won't run 12 pages, nor will the length of the book be exactly 180 pages. But at least I can tell about when I ought to be coming to an end, and keep my chapters from being too different in length.

Under this length notation I draw a line across the page, and a vertical line down the center, dividing the page in two. When I am ready to start writing, I set down the month as a heading, and under it I put the day of the week and the date when I start writing. Opposite these go the manuscript page number I actually reach that day, and the total wordage to date. Before I am through, both columns will be filled with this data, and I will have started a new page. I try to hold myself to six days of writing a week (about three hours each session), with a blank line drawn opposite the date for Sunday, when I do other things and take a break. On days when no pages are written, I set down the reason: "Stopped to plot, stopped to reread, took grandchildren on a spree," etc.

All this is for one purpose—to keep my nose to the grindstone. It is too easy, even now, for me to say, "I don't really feel like writing today." But I know that will leave a gap in my record, and all those gaps add up to *not* getting my book done on schedule. It is surprising how eager one becomes to fill those blanks with a record of work accomplished.

TITLES

Here I jot down any and all novel titles as they come to me. Sometimes I have a title before I even start working. Other times I may still be trying out and discarding titles after the book is written. I like best to be set on my title ahead of time and build it into the novel. Finding a title later may necessitate considerable rewriting.

Sometimes when nothing else about the story will move, I play around with titles, jotting down everything that comes to mind. The best ones are often the pop-into-the-mind variety, though I have searched some out by looking for headings in *Bartlett's Quotations*. For young people, a concrete title is better than an abstract one. Something specific that carries some meaning after you read the novel, and yet intrigues at first glance. You will also want something that can be easily remembered. Some words are good title words; some are not. Check your library shelves for titles that appeal to youngsters.

CHRONOLOGY

This has two sections. The first is headed *Chapters,* and when I start writing, I put down the Roman numeral of the chapter on the left, leave a space across the page, and write near the margin the number of my manuscript page on which that chapter begins. When I finish writing the chapter, I write down the number of pages in that chapter. This is useful when it comes to keeping chapter length under control, and if you know where you stand, you may want to make some changes in such lengths later.

In the space between, I will eventually write chapter titles, and these should also be intriguing to young people. I don't use chapter titles in my adult books, but they please my young mystery readers. This is another way of pulling the reader into your book when he is looking for clues that will make him want to read it.

Chapters may be regarded in the same light as the separate scenes of a short story, although a chapter may contain several scenes. Each must contribute as a whole to the major problem of the novel; each should have some minor contributing problem or problems that reach a climax near the end of the chapter. The conclusion of a chapter is important. There are several alternatives that you may use. The problem may be resolved, and you might introduce or suggest a new problem; or your main character may meet with defeat and be forced to seek a new way of achieving his or her goal; or the problem can be carried unsolved into the next chapter. Test your chapters for problems that confront the main character.

As in the short story, beware of the string-of-incidents in your novel. In a well-planned book-length story, nothing can be deleted without the collapse of the whole. When you have mere incidents strung together, it doesn't matter if one or more comes out, and the rest are pushed together. *Cause and effect build a sound plot.* Each happening grows out of what went before, and in turn results in something else. There is no cause and effect when incidents are strung in a row.

One thing to watch for in writing any book that deals with suspense or mystery—perhaps, really, in any book at all—is to make sure that your chapter ending pulls the readers along to read the next chapter, instead of making it easy for them to close the book at that point. Often I get letters from readers telling me that I've written a book that "can't be put down." Lovely! That's the trick I want to play on my readers. Study chapter endings by other writers and learn from them.

The second part under the head, *Chronology,* deals with information about characters and story events. How old was this character at this particular time? Will he be the right age to play the role you want him to play? You will need to know your characters' ages whether you give them in the story or not. Also, if there are major historic events going on at the time the novel's story takes place, you will have to make sure these are worked in at the right time. In my adult novels, the age of each character during certain past events in the book becomes very important; otherwise, they won't come out the right age at the present time in the story. In books for young people, it isn't quite so necessary to figure all this out.

With children's books these days, there is a tendency to omit the exact age of young characters, and I think this is a good idea. It used to be thought important to state ages, and we found ourselves restricted to using the older ages in any group, because younger readers would read about older children, but not the other way around. Today it may be better to show by your character's behavior generally how old he is, rather than give an exact age. Then the reader can fit in the age he likes best and feel comfortable with it.

THEME, SITUATION

Here again, there are two sections under this heading. The first, *Theme,* deals with what you mean to say through your novel. Probably it will deal with whatever you want your characters to learn. If the main character does not change at all, you have no story.

If you know what you want to say in the early planning stages, set it down under Theme as briefly as possible. You may not be sure at first, or you may have a choice among several directions the theme may take. Set anything down here that pertains in any way to the *meaning* of your story. A story that says nothing never satisfies the reader.

Sometimes finding this theme comes hard, so give yourself time and let it grow. I have heard writers say, "How do I know what I want to say until I've said it?" There can be something in this, and at times I have been well into the writing of a novel before my characters began to tell me what they wanted to say in the course of it. The important thing is not to forget that this element must be present. Sometimes when you get to one of those sticking places, you can pick up your pencil and see what may be jotted down concerning theme.

The second division in this section is *Situation*. Neither of these sections is likely to have a great deal of writing in them, so I've combined them in my notebook to save tab space.

The first writing you do for a novel may be to elaborate on the basic situation you plan to start out with. You may have been thinking about some vague idea and come up with a character, a problem, an ending—anything at all. Set it down here under Situation, in whatever detail has come to you. For me, it is usually a character facing a problem, with a background already chosen. While I am working on one novel, unconnected ideas for the next one may come to me, and I set them down in this section in order not to lose them. Situation material is what you will work with first. In the rest of the book you will elaborate on it and make it into something much more complicated.

DEVELOPMENT

This is one of the three main sections of my notebook. It could be called almost anything, but I've chosen this important section to hold all ideas concerning the *Development* of my story. Part of my job in this planning process is to *think*. When I have nothing to write, I will lie down, close my eyes, and receive whatever comes to me. In ten minutes, I am up with new ideas, and jot them down in this section. You may write these ideas in any order at all; they needn't be connected. I happen to do a lot of my plotting in pencil, because I like to think with pencil in hand, though I eventually compose on the typewriter. In my current adult novel, I have 47 handwritten pages concerning all sorts of haphazard story ideas. When one of these ideas is incorporated into the outline, or written into a chapter, I scratch it out, since I don't want to keep reading through deadwood or used-up notes. Often I will make cross-references elsewhere to some item under Development, reminding me to refer to P. 18C, or whatever. As your material grows, these references become useful, and you won't have to spend time hunting for that good thought that came to you a couple of weeks ago, but which you can't quite remember now.

Development is really the plotting section of your book, and as such is very important.

CHARACTERS

This heading is another of the Big Three in my notebook. First, I try to find names for my characters to make note of here. I use a baby book for first names, and almost any listing that has a lot of names in it for last names. I run through these, jotting down anything that appeals to me under three headings: Male, Female, Surname. Then I begin rather idly to attach names to the characters who are already stirring in my mind.

I have kept a running list of the names of the heroes and heroines of my past adult novels; otherwise I would forget and repeat them.

When I've collected a few names, I list every first letter of each first name I've chosen in one alphabetical column, and the first letter of each last name in another. I don't want to confuse the reader by using names that look alike or sound alike. It is amazing the way writers (who ought to know better) will become attached to a single letter of the alphabet, and you'll find a Sara, a Susan and a Sally in the same story. This can only lead to the confusion of the reader. Nor do you want to have too many names of the same length, number of syllables, or same rhythm. A Bob and a Job would be confusing. So would several names with "ie" endings. It is going to be hard enough for the reader to remember your characters and tell them apart; don't add to the difficulty.

Once my characters are named appropriately, I start my separate character sketches. These can run pages long, or for a minor character, cover half a page. This is where it pays off to spend a lot of your planning time. You want to know all the details possible about your story people: How they look, how they act, what they like and don't like. And also—very important—*how each one feels about all the others.* This in itself gives you wonderful character detail.

Don't make the mistake of believing that a *listing* of traits will give you a rounded character. Set down as much detail as you can about your characters—talk to yourself about them in a chatty style. Not nearly all this material will go into your book, but you'd better know more about each character than you tell the reader, if you want to make your characters real and full-fleshed. Sometimes, under the name of a character, I will write another heading: *Motivation.* This is to make sure I know why he behaves as he does. Also, this will show you conflict, clashes between one character's purpose and that of another.

OUTLINE

This is the last of your three most important sections. Under *Outline,* I *ease* into the overall planning of the story. Although I have jotted down a lot of unconnected ideas, and have written a number of pages about my characters, I don't yet know very much about my story action. Even now, when I start each book, I am inclined to look at those blank pages with a certain horror, and I wonder if I can figure out enough things to have happen (especially when I've written so much and have used up all the mystery devices I know).

At least, experience tells me that I don't have to get everything down at once. It will grow a little at a time, and somehow or other I really will think up enough action to fill a book.

My first move in this direction is to take several sheets of paper and set down Roman numerals for a rough number of chapters. I use about three to a page. In this fairly small space, I put down very briefly notes about any story action that has already come to me. In Chapter I, thus-and-so will probably happen. And perhaps something else I've thought of will fit into Chapter V. Thus, arbitrarily at first, I spread out the thin material I have, and which has been coming to me as I worked on my development section and on my character sketches. I may or may not have any idea of the ending of the book. That's why I am plotting—in order to find out how the novel will end.

Once I've put down whatever has come to me easily, I begin to work at the job of fleshing it all out. My outline begins to grow, and more and more of those blank spaces are filled in. Some chapters become so crowded with action that I run them onto additional pages, moving beyond the small space I started with.

However, I like those small spaces in the beginning, because they give me an overall picture of possible action at a glance. And they show me the blanks that need to be filled. I try to keep everything in the form of brief statements, so I save the real writing of the story for later.

Taken from my current notebook, here is an entry under Chapter XIII: C. goes to her room. Wonder what Evan will do now. Soreness from her wounded arm. Knock on the door. Judith is there. Etc.

Before I write that scene, I will probably lie down and consider it for a little while as it happens. Or if I see the scene fully by that time, I will put my fingers on the typewriter keys, and as I type, they will give me more details and action than I could think up ahead of time. (But don't count on it. Sometimes yes, sometimes no.)

One of the valuable things about this notebook system is that you don't need to keep working on one section. As you tell yourself about a character, an idea for action comes to you, and you put it into the development section. If you get an idea about a character you haven't worked out yet, put it into the Characters section. If your bit of action seems to fit into Chapter X, put it down there in your outline.

As all these sections begin to grow, you can always set the wheels of your imagination turning by reading back through what you've already written, and new ideas will flow. You give all your working hours to this notebook, and even though you're not actually writing the novel, you write in your notebook every day. Pull several pages out of your looseleaf book to work on, and move back and forth between them.

One particularly useful device that helps me with every story I write is to take small slips of paper, number them, and fasten them together with a clip. On these slips early in my planning, I set down every unanswered question that comes to me about my novel. These can become numerous before I've finished. When I sit down to work, I read through these questions and pick out several to give my concentrated attention to. When I find an answer, I set it down in the appropriate place in my notebook and scratch it out on the slip. By the time I have most of my questions scratched out and can't think of any more, I'm probably ready to write.

I say "most," because some may stump me for a very long time, and I may find the answers as I write. While I know where I'm going before I start the actual writing, I don't always know all the details about my climax scene, and questions concerning it may remain unanswered until I am nearing the end of the novel. But answers always do come. *There is always a way.*

To Be Checked

Any factual questions that come to you—things that require looking up, checking into—should be set down here so that you don't lose track of them and can give them your attention when you have time. Even in writing fiction, those things that are obviously factual must be true to life, true to place or history, or you'll get a reputation for shoddy work.

Additional

This is a very important section and can save you many headaches. As you write, you will realize again and again that something has come into the plot that will necessitate a change in some earlier chapter. If you stop everything and make the change at that moment, you will waste time and halt the forward movement of the story. You can have a compulsive desire to go back and change it, but you'd better resist it. Write it down in this section and take care of it later. Your movement ahead as fast as possible is the important thing. But you'll never remember this point if you don't keep track of it, and some of your best ideas for earlier scenes will come to you long after you have written them. You will also find holes in earlier material that you suddenly realize need to be plugged. So keep a page from this section at hand and write down anything that will need to be added, making these changes or additions later.

Another thing that can happen in the writing is a lapse of memory concerning something that went before. Did you, or did you not get that important matter in? How did you handle it? Put down a question and take care of it later. Forward movement is to be *treasured*; don't interrupt it for something you can do any time.

BIBLIOGRAPHY

If you read for research, you may need to keep track of books you have read, or need to read. This is where you keep that record.

RESEARCH

For every book I write there is special research that must be done. I have long ago used up all I know, and I have to keep dipping into new subjects to learn more. Some books I buy for my own library; others I get from the public library. In the latter case, I take notes of what may be useful to me and copy sentences or paragraphs into the *Research* section of my notebook. Such notes will be invaluable later on, because you can't hold in mind all the details of what you read. In my current research section, I have notes on Long Island history, notes on whaling, on scrimshaw, on sailing and on the designing of small boats. Also notes on adoption, since my heroine has been adopted. Only a small fraction of this material will ever be used, but I have to know more than I put into a novel or my ignorance will show. I become a minor authority while writing each book.

When the book is finished, I pull out all these reference notes and file them alphabetically under their subjects in permanent notebooks. Then if I ever want any of this material again, it will be there, waiting for me. Some subjects can be repeated over the years in totally different contexts if you write a lot.

BACKGROUND

Here I put down material collected in my travels, though usually I keep a separate, smaller notebook for that. This section can also contain odds and ends of material I collect later concerning the setting of my story. In it, I put a list of possible background scenes I could use. Change of scene (just so you don't sound like a travelogue) gives variety to your chapters, and rests and interests the reader. Listing possible scenes may help me in my plotting as well.

Also, if you happen to describe a room in a house, in an early chapter, you may want to make some brief notes of what you wrote, so that when your characters return to that room you can be sure to use the same details again. I can assure you that you won't remember, once your writing has moved on into the story. In fact, you sometimes won't be able to remember the color of your heroine's hair and eyes, or what you actually said about her when she first came onstage. Reminder notes on slips of paper are helpful, even though you have all of this detail in your notebook.

DIARY

For the most part, this section of my book stays empty now and has for years, because I don't seem to get as badly stuck as I used to—or I use different cures when I do. You may, however, find this device worth trying when you find yourself with a recalcitrant character who won't come to life. Sit him down at the typewriter and let him tell you anything he pleases in first person, as though he were keeping a diary. All sorts of unexpected detail and information can emerge. Sometimes a character can be made to jell this way.

NAMES

This has nothing to do with my current writing, though it may be used as a source for naming my characters. It stays in my book, and is a convenient place to jot down any names that come to me unexpectedly and have a special appeal. A fan letter from a young girl named Courtney caused me to enter that name on my list, and the heroine of *The Golden Unicorn* is named Courtney.

SUSPENSE TIPS

This last section of the notebook is another permanent one and contains notes I have made from various sources. There are statements about writing that I find useful and want to remember. I ought to know the "rules" by now, but a refresher course before every book I begin is helpful. So I save all these little gems to read through again, to make sure they are in my mind to be remembered.

The very last pages of my notebook contain whatever random ideas may pop into my mind for the *next* novel. They may become my *Situation* section when I start all over. Once the current book is off in the mail, I want to get to work on the next one, and it is a comforting feeling to know that the yeast is already stirring and alive. Sometimes it bubbles so fast that I become more eager to work on the next novel (where all the difficulties are not yet visible) than I am to work on the current one. Self-discipline is necessary. I know I must finish the job in hand.

So much for your notebook. The planning, the preparation mustn't go on for too long. It can become all too interesting and enjoyable just to keep on planning—much easier than writing. But you can't afford to use up too much of your time this way. In my own case, I usually receive a "signal" when it's time to write. Suddenly I feel I can do nothing more with my notebook, and the characters exert a pressure to be let out so they can start acting their roles in the story.

If this pressure becomes insistent too soon, I stop planning and write a tentative opening chapter, or opening scene. This lets the steam escape, and it gives me a good feeling of seeing my actors begin to take over onstage. Then I can go back to my notebook, where much necessary work remains to be done. Eventually, however, I *must* write, and I know that it will all go much more easily because of the preparatory work I've done.

In any case, let's say you are now ready to put words on paper. This is where you clear the decks for action. This is where you cross your friends off your list, behave rudely to anyone who calls you up during your working period, shut the door on salesmen, and become antisocial. If you can't be tough enough to do all this, you might as well accept the fact that you are going to dabble at this book for months, perhaps years to come, and that the longer this period runs, the more likely you will be to stack up odds against finishing it at all.

Now you get going. You start making the proper entries in your *Calendar* section. You hold to your schedule as long as you can. Consult your outline and your character sketches constantly to keep yourself on the right track.

Sooner or later, however, you will feel stuck. The novel turns to dust, you lose all confidence and interest in it, and you can't move ahead. Now, and *not before,* you turn back and read through what you have written, making any necessary revision as you go. Check the items in the *Additional* section and fit them in where they belong. Chances are this renewal of acquaintance with what you've written will fire you anew and furnish the impetus to go on.

However, if it doesn't, this is the point where you go back and read everything in your notebook, and consult your question slips again. With more sessions of creative thinking, new ideas begin to burgeon. Chances are that the place where you were stuck is a point in the story you hadn't thought through clearly enough. By working in your notebook once more, you will be able to overcome what was wrong, and the writing will again move ahead.

Those sticking places may occur several times before you are through, but they needn't alarm you. The flow will always return, and you'll be able to write again. In rereading, you're not wasting time, because you'll also be doing some of your necessary revision at that time.

When my first writing of a novel is finally completed, I feel a great relief, because now I can move into the part I like best. The first writing can sometimes be hard, and there is always uncertainty connected with it. Can you bring it off, can you really finish it? After fifty-five books, I still wonder about this.

But once my story is down, once that rough clay is on the armature, I can then form and shape and bring what I really want to see out of the clay.

My revision is done in pencil. Words are deleted, words written in, sentences rearranged. Sometimes new paragraphs or scenes are inserted. Then I run a penciled arrow to the margin, write "over" and set down the new passage in pencil on the back of the page. Because of my early short-story training, I sometimes have to do more expanding than cutting. And I do a great deal more revision than I did in the beginning, simply because I know how better than I used to.

By the time I am through, no one but me could ever read my manuscript. Sometimes people ask me "how many" revisions I do on a book. It doesn't work like that for me. I do a long continual revision and then finally type the whole thing to send off.

Once your book is accepted and you have an editor, don't think that's all there is to it. Undoubtedly, your editor will want more revisions from you, and you'd better oblige unless it is something that you feel you can't accept. In that case, talking it over on the phone (or in an office if you live close enough), or by mail is a good idea. I have always found editors reasonable when I was also reasonable.

In the juvenile field, it is sometimes wise to make an original copy and two carbons. One carbon is for you—an absolute *must,* to avoid possible loss in the mails. The other may be given to the artist who will do illustrations, and/or the jacket drawing.

Probably you will have nothing to say, at first, about either the art work or the jacket copy. You won't even see them until the finished book is in your hands. When you have earned your way by publishing a number of books, this may change. At the outset of your career, leave it to the experts until you become one yourself.

Before the book is ready to be published, you will be sent proofs to read and correct for typos and other necessary changes. Don't get the idea that this is your chance to re-write the whole thing. Unless you find some glaring error, don't make changes. They can be expensive, and your contract may require you to pay the cost if changes are extensive, or over a stated minimum. Mostly, you are looking for printing errors; proofreaders will be checking the proofs, too. Nevertheless, no matter how many eyes go over the pages, someone usually writes after publication to point out an error everyone appears to have missed. Be calm.

Skies will not fall. Most readers take printing errors with equanimity, though you, as author, want your book to be perfect, as do the publishers.

Of course you will feel a lovely glow when you hold that first copy of your first book in your hands. And I think that feeling of pleasure and accomplishment never entirely dies, no matter how many books you may publish. But this pinnacle of success for you—just to get published!—is only the beginning.

There will be very few ads for your novel, and you will worry about that. But children aren't reading ads, so don't be too concerned. The book trade and all those lovely librarians around the country (who will be your best customers) will be notified through *Library Journal, School Library Journal, Publishers Weekly,* and other review media. There will also be direct advertising copy, and catalogues sent to stores and libraries.

There will be some reviews, both good and bad. Don't let the good ones go to your head, or the bad ones throw you. Everyone who reads your book is likely to have a slightly different opinion. Write for *readers.* Bad reviews can wound, but they don't mean your end as a writer, if you keep working and growing.

Another matter you may wonder about is foreign sales. These are not plentiful in the juvenile field, but there may be some. In any case, your publisher will take care of sales abroad, if any. You can inquire, but this is not something you can handle yourself.

Upon publication there may be requests for you to speak to local groups, and this may be a whole new thing for you —frightening at first, but you'd better learn how if you're inexperienced. Anything that helps to publicize you and your book is worthwhile. Besides, it can be fun to get out and meet people who are interested in your writing. Librarians can be your best friends, and you'll want to work with them.

Never forget, however, that you won't be a published writer this time next year unless you get busy on another book.

14 | WRITING THE JUVENILE MYSTERY

The first requirement for the writer of mysteries, either juvenile or adult, is that he himself should enjoy this type of story. The second requirement is a thoroughly lively imagination. If you don't really like mysteries and if you lack a highly inventive mind, this field is not for you.

Good mysteries are much in demand in the juvenile book market. Children enjoy them, and librarians are eager to find better mysteries for their readers. Consequently, almost all publishers want mystery titles on their list. They know that a good mystery will be stocked by libraries all over the country and kept in print for years. Such stories are timeless, their appeal perennial for each new generation of readers.

The only catch is the fact that too many juvenile mysteries are inadequate. With more awareness on the part of the writer as to what constitutes a good mystery, better books can be published in this field. Such a book need not be a stepchild and dismissed as "just another mystery." Let's consider the qualities of a good mystery and the problems one meets in writing one.

A first and necessary step is to consult your children's librarian about the best-liked titles in the field and acquaint yourself with what is being written currently. This will give you the "feel" of the juvenile mystery as nothing else can, and it will also help you recognize overworked material and trite devices so that you can avoid them. Such reading will help you decide what age you want your characters to be and give you an idea of the length of manuscript desired. The younger the reader, the shorter the book, is usually the rule.

One of the first things to face if you mean to write mysteries for young people is the difference that exists between juvenile and adult mysteries. I don't like to use the word "taboos," because nearly every warning I give will have been ignored by one writer or another. However, I like to hold to certain principles in my own mysteries for young people, and perhaps that is one reason they are recommended by teachers and librarians and welcomed by parents.

Probably there will be no dead bodies strewn around in your mysteries. If there is one, it had better be presented innocuously and not be seen onstage. On the other hand, a murder that is "historic"—that is, one that has happened long ago—can sometimes be used. There's a pitfall for the writer here since it is all too easy to have the main story excitement in the past, while very little except curiosity is going on in the present. If your characters are in their late teens, or even in their twenties, then there is more leeway, since they are more likely to find themselves in adult adventure situations where danger is more logical, and they are old enough to deal with it. No *ugly* violence is wanted, however, and no gory details.

Certainly you must not have modern youngsters of ten or twelve capturing dangerous criminals, or risking their lives in reckless, foolish action. Desperate doings for this age character fit better into the story of a past, when young people often had to take on duties and problems beyond their years.

Sex is out. There are teen-age books that deal with the

subject honestly and realistically, but it doesn't belong in the average mystery story.

Since serious crimes must involve serious criminals, the "crimes" of the juvenile mystery are often of a minor nature. This may sound like a difficult matter to get around, but if you put your mind to it, there can be plenty that is both mysterious and exciting without being actually criminal. Often some of the young people in the story are stirring up trouble through mistaken motives, though they are not really criminals, or even juvenile delinquents.

I've heard the argument that such avoidance is not realistic, considering what children are exposed to on television. Nevertheless, there are some parents with enough strength in thumb and forefinger to turn a knob, so not all children are wallowing in the worst of television. The fact that many television programs are on the irresponsible side does not, I think, excuse the book field from setting up high standards. Fortunately, we have something to offer in the printed word that no dramatic program can provide. The reader of a story can get inside the thoughts of a character and live the experience as it is possible to do in no other entertainment field. The child who discovers this will never give up the book-reading habit. A virtue of the mystery is that it has enough excitement to pull in even the reluctant reader and get him started with books.

These "taboos" need not hinder the writer once he accepts them and looks for mystery in other directions. In writing a mystery for young people, you can let your imagination go and have a good deal of fun. The young reader is more credulous than his more sophisticated elders, more easily fooled, readier to accept small occurrences as tantalizing mysteries.

The mystery is a breeze to write, once you have it figured

out ahead of time. The hardest part is the planning, yet even that can be done without trepidation if you go about it the right way. The novice in this field may approach the mystery blankly. He has a mistaken notion that the whole mystery must somehow leap full-blown into his mind. For me, it isn't that way at all. I would find it impossible to plan the mystery part immediately and from scratch. I sneak up on it in a roundabout and painless way.

Since my hobby is collecting interesting places to write about, I usually begin with a background. I decide that the story will be set in a Hudson River town or San Francisco or Kyoto or Cape Town. An interesting setting helps, and you'll find many such settings in your own locality. The place I choose is one I have done, or intend to do, a good deal of research about, a place I know or have visited.

Once the background is settled, I forget about it for a while and think about my characters. While I always write from the viewpoint of a girl of twelve or thirteen, I see to it that there is also an important boy character of about the same age in the story. (I want both boys and girls to read my books, and from my fan mail, I judge that this happens.) In developing characters to carry my story, I think in terms of a human situation—a problem, a conflict, that might be typical of this age. There should be some serious difficulty which must be met and worked out and which would be sound and real whether the persons involved happened to be in New York, or New Orleans, or Istanbul.

In *Secret of the Samurai Sword,* I wrote about a brother and sister who didn't get along and didn't understand each other. In *Mystery of the Haunted Pool,* my heroine had to deal with a bad-tempered, self-pitying crippled boy who was spoiling things for himself and everyone else. In *Mystery of the Green Cat,* I used a step-family situation. Any human problem that interests you will do. When two or three characters involved in some sort of trouble begin to develop, I set them down in the background I'm going to write about and let one affect the other in my imagination. In *Pen to Paper*, Pamela Frankau's absorbing account of her own writing, she speaks of getting a "vibration" somewhere along the line. This is exactly what happens. Something clicks, the imagination is fired, and you're off.

But not to your typewriter—please! A good mystery must have time to grow. If you write out of that first excitement, and write too soon, I can assure you of an early demise for the whole thing. Be patient. If it's good, it will keep. If it's not, waiting will show up the bad points. Sometimes, when I get this feeling of such excitement that I am itching to get to my typewriter, I let myself write a trial opening. Usually I peter out in a few pages and don't want to go on. This is perfectly all right, since I'm not writing for real. But this exercise gives me the feeling of my characters onstage. It gives me a taste of the story. I have something solid pinned down that aids me in further development of my plan. And it also gives me some opening pages to help me over the difficult hump of getting a story started when I come to the actual writing.

In the beginning, while my characters are just stepping out of the mists and telling me their troubles, I may or may not think specifically about mystery. Any gifts from the subconscious at this time are made welcome and entered in my notebook. But I want to know something about my main character and the troublesome situation she is in before I really go to work on the mystery. Thinking first of human problems, I am sure to find meaning for my story. I want to be certain that I will say something of value to the reader along the way. The writer who thinks only in terms of action and mystery is apt to forget about this factor, and it is this very lack which makes a stepchild of the juvenile mystery. It is my conviction that a mystery can be just as good and important a story as any other kind being written for young people today.

In my books I've dealt not only with everyday human problems. I've written about racial prejudice. I've given young people a picture of Hiroshima as it is today. I've written about apartheid in South Africa. Not to bog down the story, remember, never to preach. But to give substance and meaning and value, so that the book can't be dismissed as "just another mystery." And, of course, to satisfy my own need to write about precepts I believe in. Sometimes they are world-shaking matters, sometimes not—but they always are of importance to *me*.

When the time comes to think definitely about the mystery angle in your story, let your imagination roam. Look for those vibrations again. Imagine queer, mysterious occurrences which you have no explanation for. What is going on here? Who can be up to what? Hand yourself some really colorful hunks of mystery. You don't need to know the answers; they will take a while to find.

If you think in terms of the well-worn missing will, mysterious map, or buried treasure, give it a new and unexpected twist. Never settle for the obvious.

Often an arbitrary title will lead me to the mystery. I chose *Mystery of the Green Cat* as a title before I knew what the cat was, or how it was mysterious. *Secret of the Tiger's Eye* came to me because of a ring I bought in Cape Town with a stone called a tiger's eye. That ring never got into the story, since that angle wouldn't jell. But the tiger's eye did. Thinking about the words led me to the ghost of a one-eyed tiger that was haunting a cave in Cape Town, where there are no tigers.

Any sort of an object can lead you to a mystery. The small stone statue of a man I saw in the woods near Nikko,

Japan, helped me with the mystery in *Samurai Sword.* He had his mouth open as if he were screaming, and there's a chapter in the book called "The Silent Scream." Train yourself to collect objects that can be used in mysteries. A haunting figurehead from a whaling ship, which I had seen in the Museum of the City of New York, insisted upon becoming the mysterious face in my book, *Mystery of the Haunted Pool. Mystery of the Golden Horn* is an obvious title for a mystery set in Istanbul. From it I got the entire thread of my mystery, basing it on a pin shaped like a golden horn.

Before I leave the subject of titles, a warning. Don't try to be different and original. Get "mystery" or "secret" or "ghost" into the title. Then those who are looking for mysteries can identify what you've written. The one mystery of mine that went out of print had what I considered a nice mysterious title: *The Island of Dark Woods.* Not being easily identified as a mystery in the title, however, it lagged behind my other books. Years later, it was reissued as *Mystery of the Strange Traveler,* and it has done very well. Chapters in a juvenile mystery should also be given titles. Avoid the dull and ordinary. Make your chapter titles tantalize and arouse reader interest, but don't let them give away story action and surprises. I find the best time to pick chapter titles is when I am reading through the first draft for the first time.

By all means invent an eccentric and zany character (often an adult) who may or may not be your "criminal," but who will be up to strange doings and furnish entertaining, colorful mystery for the story. The "man with the blue thumb" in *Tiger's Eye* came to me just that way, in a flash, vibrating like mad. He proved to be one of the few genuine criminals I've put into a juvenile mystery, but he's colorful in his own right and definitely sinister.

Miss Altoona, in *Haunted Pool,* is a zany nitwit who

doesn't mean to be a "criminal" but is mixed up and off on the wrong foot. My favorite juvenile zany is the girl, Adria, in *Golden Horn*. Perhaps she's my favorite of all my characters, and one who is able to create trouble all around her. A character who gets into no trouble will usually do you no good as a storyteller.

An interesting sidelight on Adria: She was frowned upon by a number of adult reviewers who found her disagreeable and unpleasant. I'm sorry they had to view her from their adult pinnacles. My readers love Adria and identify with her, and they write to tell me how good they feel when she changes at the end and learns a few things. I was really in very good company when I made her my heroine for *Mystery of the Golden Horn*. Where have we ever met a more disagreeable heroine than Frances Hodgson Burnett created in *The Secret Garden*? I still remember Mary Lennox with love and sympathy from my own childhood.

Many of the juvenile mysteries I read are far too thin. The mystery is a slim, obvious thread, and we are never sufficiently fooled along the way. Interest and excitement are low. But this needn't be. The red herring is something you can use to good effect in the juvenile field.

There will be one main, basic mystery that will be worked out at the end of the story. Crisscrossing back and forth over this main strand will be other mysterious happenings which may be fairly innocent, but which fool the main character (and the reader) for a time. A mystery must never stand still. It must develop and grow and change. All too often we find the mystery where the needle gets stuck. Some mysterious happening occurs in the first chapter, and we are curious about it. The same thing comes up again in the second chapter, and in the third. Nothing changes, and we are supposed to go on being curious. This isn't the case. Unless there are new developments, something new *hap-*

pening, we will soon get bored with mere curiosity. Your readers and your characters must be made more than curious. They must become actively *involved* in the mysterious action.

A mystery must be logically mysterious in every chapter, in every scene, and the writer must consider this and build it into his planning. If you give your characters real conflicts, real problems, a good many mysterious happenings can grow out of what they are doing. Some things will be explained as you go along, and new mysteries will crop up to take their place.

In *Tiger's Eye,* you'll find mention in the first chapter of a cave haunted by Old One-Eye, the tiger. No explanations. In later chapters, information is fed in a bit at a time until the tiger is practically onstage. In the second chapter Benita finds a mysterious circular staircase opening in the floor of her Cape Town bedroom. This isn't a real mystery —it is easily explained. But I don't explain right away. Let the reader wait till the following chapter. There are two other characters in the story besides "the villainous man with the blue thumb" who are crisscrossing back and forth, confusing the main mystery thread. By the time their doings and motives are cleared up, a bit at a time, the real mystery is moving toward the climax. This crisscrossing, however, belongs to the story. It has to do with the basic problem I'm dealing with. It is not a side road—which wouldn't do at all.

Always do the unexpected. The idea that comes to you easily is probably shopworn (vibrations excepted). Throw it back and ask your subconscious for something better. Your subconscious will do the work if you corner it and make demands.

All this is still in the planning stage. Writing is way down the line from thinking and jotting and outlining. Do a lot of thinking and jotting about your characters ahead of time. A character is not a catalogue of traits. A character is a human being with likes and dislikes, a mingling of good and bad, capable of making mistakes.

As your chapter action begins to come clear in your mind, set it down in outline form. I outline fewer chapters than I mean to write because I always write longer than I originally plan to. I keep my outline in the present tense: "Sally comes into the room and falls over the long brown bundle in the middle of the carpet." (Now what is *that* all about? If I find out, I'll have a mystery, I'm sure.) Present tense will keep you from feeling that you are actually writing the story. Don't put in all the details. This is a map you will use as a guide and a hundred unexpected details will crop up in the writing—which is as it should be.

When it comes to the writing, keep in mind your motto: A MYSTERY MUST BE MYSTERIOUS. Tantalize the reader, tease him, keep him guessing, make him ask questions and never get the right answers. Keep your mysteries growing. Don't beat one little mystery to death in every chapter until you lose your reader. He wants to be fooled.

Mysteries are fun to write as well as to read, and I enjoy surprising myself. But I do think you need a special liking and flair for this form. If you have it, your books are wanted, and they will find a great many loyal readers.

15) TO MARKET, TO MARKET!

Now your brain child is groomed and ready to go off to earn its own way. You are going to make sure it will make a good first impression. To accomplish this, it must look its best on your very first page.

You will use a fresh typewriter ribbon so that the editor will not need to struggle to figure out what you are trying to say. Use a good rag bond paper which will bear up through several mailings. However, it is not necessary to buy the heavier, more expensive 20-pound paper; I have always used the 16-pound, and it has served me well.

You will double-space, of course, and leave margins of an inch or more all around. On the first page, you should type your name and address in the upper left corner, and type the approximate number of words in your manuscript in the upper right corner. In writing for young people's magazines, where the number of words tends to be limited, it may be useful to type the exact word count, to the nearest hundred.

About a third of the way down the page, write the title, and two lines below, the word "BY," with your name on the next line. The title and author's name should be centered and look attractive on the page.

If your manuscript is not very long, you may fold it twice and put it into a long letter envelope. Have it weighed for accurate postage, and enclose a stamped, self-addressed envelope. In the case of a longer story, use a large Manila envelope and mail the manuscript without folding it. You can send a manuscript by first-class postal rates, or, more inexpensively, by book rates, in which case you must mark the envelope "Special 4th Class Rate—Manuscript."

Whether you enclose a letter to the editor depends on your having something of importance to tell him. If you have sold to other markets, that is worth mentioning, but make your remarks as brief as possible. Don't tell him how you got the idea for the story, or that it is something which really happened to your great-aunt Martha. He doesn't care. Above all, don't submit your manuscript with a letter explaining what the story is about. The story should speak for itself. And, of course, don't write to say how much you need the money. (Many writers do!)

Before you send your story to a particular editor, be sure you read several issues of the magazine from cover to cover in order not to waste the editor's time and your own by submitting a manuscript of a length and type entirely unsuited to that publication. Simple common sense should tell a writer this, but thousands of beginners send their stories off without the faintest idea of the content or editorial scope of the magazine.

Know your markets. Read your markets.

This doesn't mean that because you read a camping story in the last issue of *American Girl* you immediately send that editor another camping story. All editors are looking for variety within the scope of their own particular needs. Every magazine has its own flavor, and you must learn what that flavor is by reading many issues of the magazine.

Markets change from year to year, and your best bet is to keep up subscriptions to one or two good writers' magazines to give you up-to-date information on changes in editorial policy, and lists of the names and addresses of magazines and other publications using the type of material you want to write.

Especially if you are a beginning writer, do not avoid the more humble markets in your field. I will be forever grateful for the apprenticeship I served writing for the pulp magazines, and for the training and experience it gave me. You will benefit greatly from this kind of writing, if *in every story you write, you do the best work you are capable of at that time.* If you write carelessly and with indifference because the market does not pay very much, you will be doing yourself a decided injury. And probably you will not sell what you write. Good work cannot be done if you look down on what you're writing. It may be hard on a writer's vanity to hear this, but beginners will be lucky to sell at first even to the lowest-paying markets.

You may find poorly written stories in some of the low-paying publications (and even the better-paying ones!), but don't waste your time sneering at these stories; just try to write better ones. If you always try to better your own writing, you will soon write yourself out of the smaller markets.

Sooner or later the question of whether or not to work through an agent comes up. Beginners should market their own stories until they have a record of sales that an agent might be interested in. In most cases, at least the first book can be sold by the author as well as by an agent. Agents for the most part take care of the business end of handling manuscripts, arranging terms and subsidiary rights, and until you have substantial business for them to transact (their standard commission is ten percent of the amount paid the author), you can handle the business yourself—you do not need an agent. With or without an agent, a publisher will offer a standard contract for your first book or two—

until your sales are such that you may negotiate for better terms. Often you can continue to take care of your own affairs in the juvenile field without help from an agent for some time. As you publish more books, as contract matters become more complex, you may want to turn to a literary agent. When I began to write juvenile books, I handled them myself. But when I branched out into the adult field, an agent became necessary, and my juvenile novels, too, are now handled by my agent, whom I have relied upon for advice and guidance as well as the handling of all business matters.

It may be as difficult for you as a beginning writer to get an agent to take you on as it is to sell your first book.

Book manuscripts can be sent in cold and be assured of a first reading in many book publishing firms, and a second and more, if deserving of consideration. Query letters will almost always be read by the editors at the relatively few publishing houses that do not consider unsolicited manuscripts. Such a letter should summarize the manuscript, indicating its length and the age level for which it is intended. If you happen to know someone who knows a children's editor, the introduction may help to get you personal attention from the editor-in-chief, but it won't serve to sell a novel that editor doesn't want to buy unless it meets the company's editorial needs. Your story manuscript must sell itself. If it is good, you need not worry about its finding a place.

In the short story field, there are two methods of paying for a story—either on acceptance, or on publication. The better markets pay when they accept your story, no matter how long it may be held for publication. When it is accepted and paid for, don't expect to see it on the stands the following month. It is likely to be several months before it will see print. With small markets which pay on publication, the waiting may be long indeed, but it is better to be published somewhere than not to be published at all.

In the book field, the matter becomes more complicated, for here you will sign a formal contract, the first sight of which may dismay you completely. There are certain things you should know about contracts, though in your first one you may have to take exactly what is offered you. Fortunately, all reputable publishing houses have a standard contract which varies very little from house to house.

A 10% royalty on the list price of copies sold is the usual offer to a new author. It is not usually a good idea to accept an outright payment for all rights in the book without a provision for royalty payment on all copies sold. After you have proven that you can produce salable books repeatedly, you or your agent are in a better position to negotiate better contract terms. This will include a sliding scale, the most common practice, under which the author receives 10% royalty for sales up to 5000 copies (or sometimes 7500 these days because of the high costs of book manufacturing); 12½% up to 10,000 copies, and 15% royalty on all copies sold after that. There are variations on this scale, depending upon the success of the author and the interest the publishers have in retaining that author on their list.

The amount of the cash advance paid to an author also varies, again depending upon the importance of the writer and the strength of his negotiating position. Since advances are charged against future royalties, all you gain is having cash in hand at an earlier point—and an indication that the publisher has faith in the salability of your book. As a writer's success grows, so does the size of the advance paid, since the publisher is no longer gambling on whether the books will sell.

On your first book, an advance of at least $500 is likely.

This will be charged against royalties and deducted from the royalty statement, which is usually made twice a year.

In your contract there will usually be an option clause requiring that you show the publisher your next book. Since the publishers are taking a chance by publishing your first novel, it is only fair that they should have first look at your next book. But they are not entitled to a similar option beyond that. Options may cause a writer a great deal of grief. You cannot know in advance how matters will work out with a particular publisher. If the relationship proves unhappy or unsatisfactory, you may not want to have that publisher take your next book, but the option clause will obligate you to show them your next book. Of course, a manuscript which is rejected by the publishers immediately breaks this clause, unless they have an option on more than one book beyond the first.

Above all, beware of any publisher who asks you to help foot the bill, or to guarantee the sale of a certain number of copies. These are known to the trade as "vanity publishers," since they prey upon the writer's desire to see his book in print. They operate within the law, for they do everything the agreement requires of them. The book is printed (a small number of copies) and sent off to reviewers, who ignore it because the imprint of a vanity publisher is immediately obvious to a reviewer. The bewildered author finds that his book is in none of the stores and that it is not selling.

There is a magic word in the book business which means little to the novice, but which is the key to the entire situation. That word is "distribution." If your book does not get into the bookstores—and that doesn't mean just the stores in your hometown, but all over the country—it is not going to sell. To achieve good distribution takes a tremendous sales organization, and only the big, well-established publishing houses have this force of sales people covering the country. The vanity publisher has no such force at his command. The way he makes his money is by milking the writer. Bookstore people are a canny lot, and they know better than to touch the books of publishers who require their writers to pay part of the printing expense. Libraries also will have nothing to do with vanity publications. They buy from reviews in magazines they trust, and from publishing imprints they know not to be vanity houses. If a book is really good, it will usually sell to a reputable publisher.

However, you may not sell your first book to a big house. You may find the competition there too keen for you to break in at once, and it may be wiser to submit your manuscript to a smaller publishing house. The smaller house, as a rule, does not have the distribution enjoyed by a larger firm and consequently does not sell as many copies of a book. Nevertheless, a number of them do a very creditable job. By building up a record of consistent quality, they find their books are welcome in bookstores, even though their lists may be extremely small.

In the past few years, the market for paperback originals in the juvenile field has been opening up. Although it is still predominantly a reprint market, you should look into it to see which publishers accept original material. Write a few letters of inquiry, or consult market lists in writers' magazines. Your library may also supply you with names and addresses to query.

And now for a few words in conclusion. Perhaps I've made writing sound like very hard work in this book. If I have, it was intentional. It *is* hard work. It is not something a writer can toss off easily and then sit back and reap rewards of money and glory.

The early years of every writer are filled with discouragement and despair and disappointment. There is one hopeful thing to keep in mind, however. Progress, apparently, is made in a series of level stretches which can run along for some time before the next level is reached. I have heard artists comment similarly on their work. You plod along day after day at one level, with no sign of any improvement or progress. And then one day, almost without your realizing it, you have taken a step up and now find yourself on the next higher level. There you will remain for a time, before you move up again toward that pinnacle which will always move on ahead of you, never to be fully grasped. But how disappointing it would be to grasp it fully and have nothing more to try for. How much more fun to reach for something still ahead, always elusive.

Often in the beginning you will say, "If I could just sell *one* story!" Somehow that magic first sale looks like the opening to a road that will thereafter be easy. It isn't. Sometimes it seems as hard to sell the second, the third and the fourth story or novel as it was to sell the first. Each time you find yourself wondering if you can ever do it again. But if you keep trying, you will.

Despite my wounds and bruises, I know that I wouldn't trade my profession for any other profession in the world. A writer's office is under his hat; he can take it with him wherever he chooses to go. He is freer by far than most people in our modern civilization. He is hemmed in by no fixed horizons.

Writers often stay young more successfully than other mortals do. Perhaps it is because no person with a keen and lively interest in life can really grow old. And when you are a writer, your senses never atrophy. Every scene, every person you meet, everything that is said and done around you, is grist for your ever-active mill.

This is particularly true of those who write for children. When you are kept busy seeing everything about you through young, excited eyes, there is no time to be bored. Those who are ever interested are ever young.